KW-477-600

HIGH POLITICS IN THE LOW COUNTRIES

For Yasemin

90 0548071 5

WITHDRAWN
FROM
UNIVERSITY OF PLYMOUTH
LIBRARY SERVICES

SEVEN DAY LOAN

This book is to be returned on
or before the date stamped below

− 3 OCT 2003

UNIVERSITY OF PLYMOUTH

PLYMOUTH LIBRARY

Tel: (01752) 232323
This book is subject to recall if required by another reader
Books may be renewed by phone
CHARGES WILL BE MADE FOR OVERDUE BOOKS

High Politics in the Low Countries

An Empirical Study of Coalition Agreements in Belgium and The Netherlands

ARCO I. TIMMERMANS
University of Twente,
The Netherlands

ASHGATE

© Arco I. Timmermans 2003

All rights reserved. No part of this publication may be reproduced, stored in a retrieval system, or transmitted in any form or by any means, electronic, mechanical, photocopying, recording or otherwise without the prior permission of the publisher.

Published by
Ashgate Publishing Limited
Gower House
Croft Road
Aldershot
Hants GU11 3HR
England

Ashgate Publishing Company
Suite 420
101 Cherry Street
Burlington, VT 05401-4405
USA

Ashgate website: http://www.ashgate.com

British Library Cataloguing in Publication Data
Timmermans, Arco
   High politics in the Low Countries : an empirical study
   of coalition agreements in Belgium and the Netherlands
   1.Coalition governments 2.Coalition governments - Belgium -
   Case studies 3.Coalition governments - Netherlands - Case
   studies
   I.Title
   324.2'492'013

Library of Congress Cataloging-in-Publication Data
Timmermans, Arco, 1964-
   High politics in the Low Countries : an empirical study of coalition agreements in
   Belgium and the Netherlands / Arco Timmermans.
      p. cm.
   Includes bibliographical references and index.
   ISBN 0-7546-1559-6 (alk. paper)
      1. Belgium--Politics and government--1951-1993. 2. Belgium--Politics and
   government--1993- 3. Coalition governments--Belgium. 4. Netherlands--Politics and
   government--1945- 5. Coalition governments--Netherlands. I. Title.

   JN6165 .T56 2003
   328.492'0769--dc21
                                                                          2002190862
ISBN 0 7546 1559 6   ✓

Printed and bound in Great Britain by Antony Rowe Ltd, Chippenham, Wilts.

Contents

UNIVERSITY OF PLYMOUTH

Item No. 9005480715

Date − 3 SEP 2003 2

Class No. 320 . 9492 TIM
Cont. No.

PLYMOUTH LIBRARY

List of Tables

Preface

On 15 May 2002, the most dramatic parliamentary elections since 1945 took place in the Netherlands. A week before the elections, the charismatic leader of a new party, the Lijst Pim Fortuyn, was assassinated. This party was as a protest party challenging the three party coalition that had governed the country for eight years. This coalition controlled 97 of the 150 seats in the Second Chamber, the lower house of parliament, but after election day only 54 seats were left. The Lijst Pim Fortuyn, which was formed only a few months before the elections, took 26 seats and became the second largest party.

These elections shocked the established parties and marked the beginning of a government formation that 'would make things different'. Promises were made about a change in the style of politics: less 'wheeling and dealing' behind closed doors, and more openness. The formateur's party, the CDA (Christian Democrats), declared that the new coalition parties should make as few precommitments as possible – the coalition agreement should be not longer than one page, cabinet ministers should have more autonomy than before, and parliament should be more critical and less constrained by the mores of coalition discipline.

When after two months of negotiations the new government composed of CDA, VVD (Liberals) and Lijst Pim Fortuyn took office, it had a coalition agreement of 45 pages, but with many vague intentions to which only few ministers had contributed. The relatively short negotiations had been surrounded by secrecy – even to candidates for a cabinet portfolio. Several newly appointed ministers expressed policy ambitions in contradiction to the coalition agreement, and this led to anxiety among the parliamentary leaders who had negotiated the deals. Moreover, the Lijst Pim Fortuyn was barely a political party and became an arena of internal discord and leadership rivalry. This new coalition government led by a relatively unexperienced prime minister had invested in establishing policy agreement before taking office, but many doubts existed about the stability of this political fundament.

Coalition agreements between political parties taking office together are the central subject of this book. A large discrepancy exists between the broad attention for coalition agreements among political and social actors and in the media in countries with coalition governments, and the rather limited attention for this subject in the political science literature. This book explores the roles of coalition agreements in politics. Many of the ideas about this subject developed in discussions with Jean Blondel and Rudy B. Andeweg, at different locations of which the European University Institute in Florence has been most important to me. I would also like to thank the members of the research team on Actors and Institutions in Western European Parliamentary Democracies, who in one way or another helped to streamline my ideas about coalition politics. Peter Scholten has been a great research assistant during the final stage of this book project.

Finally, I would like to thank all of my friends for their support during my research. In particular, I remember my stay at Amasya in May 2002 – thanks Ümmü

Gülsüm Cegerek-Matpan, your hospitality and warmth are invaluable to me. To your daughter, Yasemin Cegerek, my partner for life, I dedicate this book.

Enschede, August 2002

Chapter 1

Government Formation and Beyond: An Empirical Study

One of the most obvious questions someone could ask about coalition governments is what these governments do. Since coalitions began to be studied in the early 1960s, however, this question has hardly been addressed in a systematic way. Most of the time, attention in coalition research was focused on the formation of coalitions and on their end, and both were the subject of deductive theory building based on the assumptions of rational choice.

The most extensively studied element of coalition politics was government formation. Theories on this subject evolved from variations of Riker's straightforward *size principle* (1962) to sophisticated approaches dealing with bargaining strategies and the different kinds of results they may yield. The other challenge that drove theorists in the same intellectual corner was to explain the stability and duration of coalitions (see Warwick, 1994 and Laver and Shepsle, 1996 for useful discussions of this literature). There has been attention for aspects of the life of governments, but this has formed a research world apart, the domain of country specialists and comparativists going into entirely different questions not specific to coalition governments (see for example Blondel, 1988; Blondel and Müller-Rommel, 1993; Blondel and Cotta, 1996). The consequence of this remarkable research landscape is that the answers to the question what happens during the life of coalition governments still contain a good deal of speculation.

Linking Coalition Birth to Life: Coalition Agreements

Bargaining between parties is a key element of coalition government. Interparty bargaining never stops, and this is an intriguing point for students of coalition governments. As said, government formation often is taken as the focal point in studies of coalition bargaining. But if government formation is the point of departure in analysis, it need not also be the end point. Coalition agreements link government formation to government life. Parties all calculate their policy payoffs before government arrangements are definitive and ratified, but these payoffs concern intentions that begin to have a substantive meaning only after the government has taken office. Then, bargaining either may no longer be necessary because all policy disputes were settled, or bargaining may go on, and usually this is what happens.

From country reports we know that there is variation in the time and energy devoted to policy negotiations during government formation. This means, that coalition agreements, the written documents containing all kinds of intentions on coalition policy, may also vary between coalitions and between countries.

1

A minimum position with respect to the actual meaning of such coalition agreements is taken by Laver and Schofield in their book *Multiparty Government* (1990). They argue that interparty policy negotiations have a symbolic meaning, confirming the common viewpoints rather than that they are organized to establish agreement on policy conflicts. If parties want to form a coalition, they argue, why would they bother in advance about policy conflicts and constrain themselves by formulating all kinds of commitment? Luebbert (1986) asserts that policy negotiations during government formation have mainly intraparty purposes. Party leaders are seen to use these negotiations to keep their followers happy.

But does this minimum position provide an adequate picture of the process and results of policy negotiations in coalition formation? Policy negotiations during government formation also can be seen in a different way. In this alternative view, less common in coalition research and first presented by Peterson et al. (1983), government formation is an arena *par excellence* for bargaining on coalition policy. The authors illustrate their argument with examples from Belgium and the Netherlands, two typical coalition systems. In the government formation arena, discussions between party leaders and other party spokespeople can be more informal and are constrained less by institutional rules of policy making, and they are also less exposed to the broader public. This may facilitate making deals on coalition policy, though negotiators need to keep an open line with followers to avoid problems of legitimacy later on.

Thus conceived as a bargaining opportunity, parties are likely to focus their attention in government formation on a limited set of issues – they emphasize the subjects that are most salient to them. A question following from this is to what degree of specificity and how persistently policy viewpoints are upheld. In the first comparative empirical study of coalition governments in Western European countries, Browne and Dreijmanis (1982: 349–250) depicted policy negotiations as a process 'to apportion influence among the partners and establish an initial condition of programmatic unity among them.' Parties may use principles and ideological profiles as the input for such negotiations, but they must translate this to more or less concrete policy positions. For this reason, parties may concentrate on issues that are salient and on which they have disagreement. Policy conflicts not only arise during government formation; they also may have emerged earlier, during the previous government and even may have caused coalition collapse. Particularly in this last situation, parties mistrust each other and will feel a need to make clear deals.

Aim and Organization of This Book

The second view of policy bargaining is based on observations about politics in the Netherlands and Belgium, but it may have more general relevance. The question that follows when taking manifest policy disputes in government formation as the point of departure, is to what extent such conflicts are really resolved before the government takes office. And how does this become visible in the coalition agreement as the output of government formation? Bargaining may result in compromises, but these may take different forms and be negotiated one by one or in packages in which different issues are linked. And the deals or compromises may be substantive or procedural, specific or general, and clear or ambiguous. The political formulas chosen by parties reflect the degree to which dispute was resolved during government formation.

When agreements made on controversial issues are on the government agenda, different things may happen. They may be implemented directly or become the object of further coalition bargaining. They even may be forgotten, though this is not likely for issues that were salient to most or all parties. Deals may increase efficiency of decision making by removing the conflict element, but they may also generate new trouble in the coalition. Thus, coalition agreements may have different effects during the life of governments. These effects may relate to the types of deals, but they may also be determined by the ways in which coalitions organize the policy making process. Thus far, none of these possible effects nor their conditions have been investigated in coalition research.

Such an empirical investigation is the aim of this study. The general point of departure is that coalition agreements link government formation to government life. The nature of negotiations on coalition agreements and their results may vary between countries with different party systems and institutional rules influencing government formation. For this reason, the first thing to consider is how large this variation in the practice of writing coalition agreements is in Western Europe. Where do we find coalition agreements? How long are these documents, and how is variation in these properties related to coalition features, or to country characteristics? Recent empirical work on the general features of coalition agreements in different countries helps to answer this question, which is central in chapter 2.

Once this *tour d'horizon* of coalition agreements is done, it is possible to move on to more specific questions about the functions of agreements. What is written down in coalition agreements is likely to reflect the way in which parties perceive policy bargaining during government formation. As said, in coalition research, two opposite views of policy agreements exist, and chapter 3 presents these views in the literature on coalition politics. What are the possible functions of coalition agreements? And what conditions may be relevant for performance of these functions during the life of governments? Here, the key issue is the problem of enforcement. In this chapter, the central concepts and a number of hypotheses on effects of types of deals are presented.

Chapter 4 contains an introduction to the case studies dealing with the questions on effects of coalition agreements. A case study approach is chosen in this book to explore the variation in the ways coalition parties have dealt with controversial issues in government formation and beyond. Five coalition governments are studied: two from Belgium in the 1970s, two from the Netherlands in the 1980s, and one other Dutch coalition in the 1990s. For each coalition government, the disputed issues and the deals on them in government formation are analyzed, the effects of these deals in terms of conflict prevention and implementation, and the favourable or unfavourable conditions for enforcement that may help explain effects. Except for impressionistic accounts in the media, we still know little about the effects of coalition agreements in these two countries, and for this reason each case is considered extensively. This is done in the chapters 5 through 9.

In chapter 10, these findings from the cases are taken together, and the patterns in types of deals, their effects, and enforcement conditions are examined. What types of arrangements on policy conflicts ensue in what policy fields? Is there a pattern to be found in the performance of the substantive functions of coalition agreements? Are there differences between cases, or between countries – what government was most successful and which one was least able to keep the peace and enhance efficiency of decisions making through the coalition agreement? If the effects were failure, in what arenas has this failure occurred? And what can be said about the different conditions that were assumed to be relevant to enforcement? What is the interplay between structural properties of coalitions and processes within these coalitions?

There are thus many questions to be asked about coalition agreements, and this book will not give definitive answers. This study is meant to begin addressing empirical questions about coalition governments beyond their formation, and to show that a focus on the high politics of controversial issues is a useful one. The empirical scope of the study is Belgium and the Netherlands, the two low countries with a tradition of coalition governments. The political tradition in both these countries is one of accommodation and consensus (Lijphart, 1968; 1999), of which coalition agreements are a more recent expression. None the less, as the next chapter will show, coalition governments are on the rise in Western Europe, and indeed also in many countries outside Europe. This may indicate that the theme and approach developed in this book may have a more general relevance for the study of multiparty government.

Chapter 2

Bargaining, Policy, and Coalition Agreements

Introduction

Almost all Western European countries, and an increasing number of countries outside Western Europe, have experience with coalition government. Coalition government is a form of government in which two or more political parties form the executive – if possible until the next elections. Spain and the United Kingdom are the only countries in Western Europe without a record of coalition government since 1945. In all other Western European countries, coalition governments have been in office for some or most of the time. In Austria, Belgium, Finland, France, Germany, Iceland, Italy, Luxembourg, the Netherlands and Switzerland, multi party government prevails. Luxembourg, the Netherlands and Switzerland never had a single party government since 1945.

These government coalitions do not always control a stable parliamentary majority. Minority coalition governments emerge in most of the countries just mentioned. In countries such as Denmark and Finland they are even frequent. Minority coalitions may be the result of a government crisis and be given caretaker status, or they may be formed after elections and be meant to survive until the end of the Constitutional term in office. In the second case, they are vulnerable because they depend on the passive or active support of one or more other parties in parliament. Such coalitions need to build majority support, and this can be done ad hoc or through a support agreement put together before or after the coalition is formed. This was done for example in 1996 in Spain, when the People's Party formed a single party minority government after the Social Democrats were defeated in the elections. Support agreements may reduce political risks, but they do not always give the government coalition a stable majority. Another situation occurring in Western Europe is that a party with an absolute majority takes other parties on board. Such large coalition governments are less vulnerable, but they also are more exceptional. Thus, coalition governments emerge in majority and minority situations, and they consist of parties controlling a stable majority in parliament, or they are composed of parties that need to construct such a majority during their term in office.

Coalition agreements, the documents containing coalition policy intentions, are less widespread than coalition governments. Not all coalition governments have such agreements. Where and under what conditions are coalition agreements made in multi party systems?

This chapter deals with this question. It is about the context in which coalition agreements emerge. It presents insights from research on coalition governments that are useful for drawing up this context – the countries and cases in which parties negotiate a coalition agreement. Some of these insights are based on theory, and some are empirical. The first section gives a brief overview of coalition research from its embryonic stage onwards. The conclusion to be drawn from this overview is clear: theoretical contributions have much to say about the systemic context of coalition bargaining and about coalition government formation, but they do not really tell us what happens during the life of coalition governments, and they are even more silent about coalition agreements and the role they may play. Section two provides the context of coalition agreement production in theoretical terms: it is about properties of bargaining systems in which parties coalesce. Section three takes these properties as a point of departure in an empirical *tour d'horizon* of coalition agreements. What countries have coalition agreements, and what are the features of agreements across these countries? For these questions, findings from recent comparative empirical work on coalition governance are useful.

A Brief History of Coalition Research

Given the prominence of coalition government in Western Europe, it is not surprising that this type of government has obtained much attention from political scientists. This attention emerged in the 1960s, and was strongly driven by game theory and rational choice theory. The main object of theoretical attention was the formation of coalition governments, followed by coalition stability. Initially, the focus was on the set of possible coalitions that could be formed on the basis of numerical conditions – the size of parties represented in parliament. The underlying assumption borrowed from rational choice theory was that parties try to form party combinations that are as small as possible, and involve not more power sharing than needed to control a majority. In such coalitions, each party seeks to maximize its gains from political trade. Such coalitions could take different forms. First, they could be *minimal winning*, that is, be a combination in which each party is indispensable for a parliamentary majority (Riker, 1962). Or they could be *minimum winning* – the smallest possible combination beyond 50 percent of the parliamentary seats (Gamson, 1961; Riker, 1962). Or they could contain the minimal number of parties necessary for a parliamentary majority (Leiserson, 1968).

These size based approaches appeared not to be very successful in explaining coalition formation and duration in the real world. Not more than about one third of all coalitions that *were* formed, could be accounted for by any of these theories. A key point of critique was that they ignored ideology and policy, and more refined theories incorporating these elements emerged in the early 1970s. The central characteristic of this second generation of coalition theory was that the positions of parties were mapped onto a policy dimension, the Left-Right scale. In one theory, the assumption was that coalitions are not only minimal winning but also contain parties that are each other's ideological neighbours (Axelrod, 1970). In another theory, the prediction was that combinations occur in which the partners have a minimal ideological range – reducing the distance between policy intentions that the coalition parties need to bridge (De Swaan, 1973). These contributions increased the empirical relevance of coalition theory. In addition to coalition formation, scholars considered coalition stability and duration. The theoretical assumptions were largely similar to the ones guiding coalition formation theory, and were based on size and ideological attributes of coalitions. Coalitions of minimal size and minimal ideological heterogeneity were expected to be most durable (Dodd, 1976; Sanders and Herman, 1977; Warwick, 1979). Thus, two different phenomena, coalition formation and coalition duration, were accounted for by essentially the same factors.

In the 1980s, these theories in turn were challenged. Though the explanatory power of deductive coalition theory focusing on government formation had increased, it was beginning to be considered too formal and static. According to this critique, coalition politics was depicted too much as a game played at one fixed point in time, and the end as something that 'just happened', without being clear why for example on Friday 13th and not at some other moment. What happens with coalition governments was seen to be not just a matter of their structural attributes (size, ideological homogeneity) but also of shocks and unpredictable events (Browne, Frendreis and Gleiber, 1986). Thus more attention was given to the *dynamic* character of coalition politics (Browne and Franklin, 1986; Strøm, 1984; 1990). A second point of critique was that the assumption of parties as utility maximizing 'office-seekers' could not explain the construction of minority governments and governments of more-than-minimal winning size (surplus majority coalitions) (Budge and Laver, 1986; Laver and Schofield, 1990). These types of governments have emerged in most countries with coalition governments. Parties increasingly were considered to be multi-motivational; they are driven by the desire to get into office, but also by policy considerations and electoral prospects. Particularly the concept of policy was seen to need operationalization; parties may have ideological bases, but in the reality of coalition politics, they deal and often struggle with issues that may unite or divide them. A third point of attention was the assumption that parties are unitary actors. Parties increasingly were seen as arenas of competition – a distinct level of relationships within coalitions with significance for the formation and stability of coalition governments (Luebbert, 1983; 1986). Empirical underpinnings of these points of critique were the country studies in several edited volumes on coalition governments in Western Europe, which all involved more facets of coalition politics than in the theoretical contributions (Browne and Dreijmanis, 1982; Bogdanor, 1983; Pridham, 1986).

These developments towards a broader and more differentiated perspective in the study of coalition governments continued in the 1990s. The most significant theoretical and analytical innovations were made with respect to the role of policy in coalition building. First, coalition bargaining increasingly was seen to involve more than one policy dimension and take place in an institutional context that may differ across countries. This is what country specialists doing empirical studies of coalition governments in Europe were claiming since the 1980s, and their insights were taken into account also in the more theoretically oriented literature. Multidimensional bargaining on policy was conceptualized and related to the question under what conditions a policy equilibrium between parties was possible – or impossible (Baron, 1991; 1993; Schofield, 1993). More substantive empirical work was done on party policy positions and the policy profiles of coalition governments (Laver and Budge, 1992; Laver and Hunt, 1992; Klingemann, Hofferbert and Budge, 1994). Institutional conditions for coalition bargaining also were given more systematic attention (North, 1990; Strøm, Budge and Laver, 1994; Tsebelis, 1995; Scharpf, 1997). The second innovation in coalition research was made by Laver and Shepsle (1990; 1994; 1996), who focused on the role of cabinet ministers in policy making. Their assumption was that policy making within governments is decentralized, with cabinet ministers enjoying large autonomy in policy making. In this approach, the allocation of cabinet portfolios is a key determinant of government policy. A confrontation of this approach with experiences in Western European countries however shows that it underestimates the centralizing force of interparty relationships within coalition governments and the mechanisms that these parties design for mutual control (several chapters in Laver and Shepsle, 1994).

Thus, since the 1960s, coalition research has developed from a small playground for rational choice theorists to an important subfield in political science in which different approaches – deductive and inductive – exist. Yet, coalition theory is only slowly beginning to meet the empirical world of coalition politics in Europe. The focus long has been on coalition formation and since recently is shifting to coalition life – to what goes on within coalition governments after they are formed. This shift is taking place in the aforementioned theoretical work on portfolio allocation done by Laver and Shepsle, but it is more visible in the comparative empirical assessments of internal structures of governments and government-party relationships by Blondel and associates (1993; 1996), and particularly in the comparative work on coalition governments conducted by Müller, Strøm and associates (2000; forthcoming). The team of Müller and Strøm has systematically compared properties of elements of coalition governments such as the formation, the portfolio distribution and policy programmes, governance mechanisms, government duration and causes of termination, and electoral performance (Strøm, Müller and Bergman, forthcoming). This work is likely to inform coalition theory in the future.

Bargaining Systems and Coalition Politics

Coalition politics takes place within a bargaining system of some kind. A bargaining system is an analytical model for representing relationships between relevant parties – within and outside the government. A political party is relevant if it has the potential to participate in a government. The bargaining system is the context of collective action – cooperative or noncooperative – and it influences party behaviour, ad hoc and strategic. As such, the bargaining sytem context structures the way in which coalition governments are formed, maintained, and end.

A significant element of a bargaining system is the policy space. A policy space is made up of one or more policy dimensions – sets of theoretically possible policy preferences. A policy dimension usually represents a political cleavage, which can be socio-economic, religious, ethno-linguistic, or other. These cleavages often constitute the historical basis of parties, and new schisms or the disappearance of a cleavage may lead to party realignments. Political cleavages not only have an effect on the party system in a structural sense – in terms of its size and form – but also on bargaining relationships within the system. Bargaining relationships between parties thus depend, among other things such as political reputations, on the position that parties take on the salient policy dimension(s). Such positions are not frozen and fixed; parties move in the policy space in different directions over time, sometimes radically but mostly in an incremental way.

Types of Bargaining Systems and Variation in Coalition Politics

Laver & Schofield (1990: 110–137) distinguish between three types of bargaining systems: unipolar, bipolar and multipolar systems. All three are multiparty systems. Unipolar systems contain one large party and a number of (much) smaller parties. This situation exists for example in Ireland, Norway and Sweden, where the largest party can dominate the government or even be the single government party. Alternations in government often consist of the single largest party being replaced by a coalition, not always a majority, of the smaller parties. Coalition governments thus emerge, but unipolar systems are not typical coalition systems. Coalition governments are more frequent in bipolar systems, which contain two large parties (the two poles) and a third and possibly a fourth much smaller party. This is the situation in Germany and Austria, where different kinds of coalitions have emerged (but Austria also has had single party governments). In multipolar bargaining systems, size differences between relevant parties are relatively limited, and it does not happen often that one party controls an absolute majority in parliament. Examples are Belgium, Finland and the Netherlands, where governments mostly or even always are coalitions. The dominance in office of the Christian Democratic party in Belgium and the Netherlands however reduced the meaning of multipolarity (Warwick, 1994). Both systems became more truly multipolar in the second part of the 1990s, when the Christian Democrats ceased to be the indispensable party in coalition building.

Though the formal Constitutional design of a country and rules of the game within policy making bodies such as parliament and the cabinet also play a part, the type of bargaining system is important for variation in coalition politics across countries. The most outstanding difference seems to be that between multipolar systems compared to unipolar and bipolar systems, a point emphasized by Laver and Schofield when presenting the typology of bargaining systems. They argue that in multipolar systems, parties are most sensitive to election results and to changes in policy positions, have incentives to renegotiate coalition deals, and for this reason reduce the likelihood that coalition governments survive (1990: 158). There is empirical evidence for this assertion about government duration since 1945 (Laver and Schofield, 1990: 100; Müller and Strøm, 2000: 585), as well as for the assertion that inter-party conflict is a major cause of early government termination (Nousiainen, 1993: 272; Müller and Strøm, 2000: 586). But this is not the clearest point of evidence, since in the Netherlands and increasingly also in Belgium, governments have become more stable (Timmermans and Andeweg, 2000: 390–391; Dewinter, Timmermans and Dumont, 2000: 320–321). The features that make these two countries more typical as multipolar systems relate to coalition building and to the properties of coalitions. First, there are more bargaining rounds involving different sets of parties, and coalition building also takes more time. This pattern is continued in the 1990s (Müller and Strøm, 2000: 570). Laver and Schofield (1990: 162) originally called aborted coalition building attempts 'failures', but coalition formation is a process of selection in which subsequent alternatives do not necessarily become less preferred.

Second, coalition governments in Belgium, Finland and the Netherlands contain more parties (more than three on average) and also show more variation over time in the party composition of governments (Strøm, 1990: 246–269; Müller and Strøm, 2000: 561). In addition, the governments formed consist of parties that are less often each others ideological neighbours on one single dimension of policy (the Left-Right dimension) than in other countries. This does not mean that policy is unimportant during coalition formation, but that at least one other policy dimension is involved. It means also that the coalition parties must deal with policy heterogeneity among them in one way or another. The long duration of coalition formation involving multiple rounds of bargaining may be features of political theatre, but they may also indicate that parties invest in negotiating some kind of agreement on policy, to reduce the costs of political transactions during the life of the government. Let us turn to this more specific element of coalition politics.

Bargaining on Coalition Policy

As said, the bargaining system in a country contains a policy space in which party positions lead to particular bargaining relationships between them. Such positions are relevant throughout the life cycle of coalition governments, of which government formation is the first stage. In most countries, and most clearly in multipolar systems which have the largest number of relevant parties, the policy space consists of at least two policy dimensions on which parties take a particular profile. Research on the dimensionality of party systems – and thus on the policy space in which parties interact – shows variation in the way policy dimensions are operationalized, and how the salience of a policy dimension is measured. Approaches vary by taking either policy platforms and programmes or expert judgements as a basis, and they also have gone different paths in modelling party positions. Policy dimensions are defined in terms of ideological cleavages or seen as distinct policy fields in which parties explicate particular preferences. When party positions in different fields covary, these fields constitute a policy dimension (see for example Budge, Robertson and Hearl, 1987; Laver and Budge, 1992; Laver and Hunt, 1992).

In this book, I use a level of analysis as close as possible to concrete policy issues on which parties take positions – and on which they may be in conflict when building a coalition government. For this reason, it is important to consider the nature of bargaining relationships among parties in the fields in which parties take positions, and determine the extent to which these fields are generally salient, or are salient to some but not all parties involved in coalition politics. If parties give different weights to policy fields in their electoral campaigns and in policy making, a different bargaining situation exists than when all parties consider all matters to be equally important.

Types of Bargaining Relationships

A useful and non-formal representation of these possible situations is provided by Luebbert (1984; 1986) in his comparative study of government formation. According to Luebbert (1986: 65), each party has a particular *limit of tolerance*:

The hypothesized limit (of tolerance) applies to the least favorable relationship that exists between the two parties within their entire set of relevant preferences. If the parties have convergent preferences on one issue and divergent (...) preferences on another, the bargaining relationship is divergent (...). The *formateurs* (of one party) will always be willing to proceed to the limit of tolerance, but not beyond it. The government that emerges is, in this view, a by-product of the prevailing constellation of bargaining relationships and the systematically determined consequences that the *formateurs* find attached to different levels of tolerance.

In Luebbert's approach, parties may take clear positions on all policy dimensions, or in all fields, but they may not only agree or differ in these positions but also persist more strongly in their position in one field than in another. A party may even be indifferent about policy on one or more issues. Luebbert calls this a situation of tangential bargaining relationships (1986: 62–63). This notion is close to what is called the 'saliency approach' of party competition (Budge and Farlie, 1983) but it is not advanced as a general proposition about party behaviour. Tangential bargaining relationships allow parties to make deals relatively easily; party A may accept B's preference for an increase in defence spending if B accepts A's wish for higher penalties for exceeding the maximum speed on motorways.

But usually, coalition bargaining is not that simple. Parties may, and often do, care about issues in multiple fields, not least because they need to be credible when engaging in coalition formation. They need to take a stand on all issues. Thus parties have also convergent and, most importantly, divergent bargaining relationships – they may agree or disagree on policies for issues that matter to them all. Situations of policy divergence are the cases of real negotiation (in which also tangential issues may be involved), and the possible results identified by Luebbert are explicit or implicit compromises (1986: 62–63). Explicit compromises contain unilateral or mutual and substantive concessions. Implicit compromises are agreements to disagree, and these may take the form of procedural arrangements such as postponements or statements which are sufficiently general or vague that no party will feel that its preferences are ignored. Thus, explicit compromises commit the coalition parties to substantive policies, and implicit compromises contain commitments to some kind of procedural agreement or contain vague and weak commitments.

The reasons why parties formulate an explicit compromise or resort to an implicit compromise vary. This depends for example on the nature and definition of the issue, which may involve viewpoints that are more or less easy to compromise. If issues have a high ideological content, preferences may be incompatible, and substantive explicit compromises difficult to reach. Strategic considerations may also play a part. A party may for example want to prevent that one or more of its government partners form an ad hoc legislative coalition on an issue, and build this prevention in by formulating a rule of coalition discipline on the issue. Another reason why parties may be reluctant to make clear commitments is the existence of internal party divisions.

Thus, in a bargaining system containing different policy dimensions or fields, the bargaining relationships between parties determine the collective agenda of coalition government formation. Particularly divergent bargaining relationships are important, because they determine in part or even entirely who will join the new government (this was the central point in Luebbert's analysis of government formation). Also tangential relationships are likely to play a part in the deals that parties make when taking office. The extent to which this happens is likely to vary across countries, and this may become manifest in the proliferation of coalition agreements, and in the contents of these agreements made during coalition formation.

Results of Policy Bargaining: Coalition Agreements

Research attention for coalition agreements is very recent, but the practice of putting such agreements together is well established in most countries with multi party governments. In this section, I give a brief account of the existence and the features of coalition agreements in Western Europe, and I relate the emerging empirical patterns to the properties of governments and bargaining systems. To what extent does the type of coalition and the bargaining system context make a difference to the coalition agreement as an output of government formation?

What is a Coalition Agreement?

A coalition agreement is an agreement made by two or more parties during government formation. This is done not only before the government takes office, but mostly also before the distribution of cabinet portfolios is determined. Coalition agreements may be more or less substantive; they may contain policy intentions, procedures for decision making and other kinds of collective action, and distributions of portfolios, delimitation of jurisdictions and spoils may also be incorporated into agreements. I consider coalition agreements that are formalized and written, not informal and oral agreements. They may be published, but this is not always the case. Often, coalition agreements constitute the basis of what is presented officially by the prime minister when the new government takes office, the government programme or declaration. Coalition agreements are made *for* the new government, that is, they are drafted by party spokespersons who may or may not become a minister.

Coalition agreements differ also from support agreements made between parties within a government and one or more external parties for obtaining majority support in parliament. Support agreements usually contain a limited number of matters on which commitments are made, but they may also be single issue agreements made with different parties. Both types of agreements are intended to reduce uncertainty about majority support for government policies, but they do this in different ways. The distinctive element of support agreements is thus the involvement of external parties – something that coalition agreements usually are meant to prevent.

Occurrence of Coalition Agreements

For obvious reasons, coalition agreements are more frequent in countries where coalition governments prevail. But typical coalition systems such as Belgium, Germany and the Netherlands did not always have coalition agreements, and in countries with less coalition experience, agreements emerge often or even always when a coalition government is formed.

This becomes clear from a recent empirical analysis of coalition agreements as an element of coalition governance in thirteen Western European countries conducted by Müller and Strøm (2000; 2001). Müller, Strøm and associates show for example that in Norway and Sweden, all coalition governments had a coalition agreement, and in Ireland this was nearly always the case, while in these three countries single party governments were more frequent. Belgium, the Netherlands and Germany have seen coalition agreements since the late 1950s and early 1960s (2000: 573–574). This last development is a more general one observed by Strøm and Müller: gradually, coalition agreements have become more usual in situations of coalition government since 1945. In the 1940s, only one third of all coalition governments had an agreement, whereas in the 1990s this was the situation in 81 percent of the cases (2001: 23).

Strøm and Müller (2001) have further explored relationships between the occurrence of coalition agreements and, as independent variables, the properties of cabinets and characteristics of the bargaining system context, but the findings from this exploration do not point clearly in one particular theoretical direction. The clearest points in their analysis are that majority governments have more often a coalition agreement than minority governments, and that the likelihood of a coalition agreement is higher if the coalition is minimal winning and contains a strong party (Strøm and Müller, 2001: 15–16). The types of bargaining systems presented earlier in this chapter do not relate strongly to the emergence of coalition agreements. Thus, unipolar systems such as Norway, Sweden and Ireland, the bipolar systems of Austria and Germany, and the multipolar systems of Belgium, Finland and the Netherlands all have coalition agreements, and they occur most frequently in the 1980s and 1990s. This suggests that coalition agreements have institutionalized as a part of (majority) government formation, and that this institutionalization has taken place simultaneously in most Western European countries with an experience in coalition government.

Features of Coalition Agreements

Coalition agreements may be brief and made overnight, or they may be lengthy documents drafted with fervour by party delegations. The composition of party delegations varies between countries as well as within countries over time. In most countries, parliamentary spokespeople are involved, and negotiations may be organized by forming work groups containing area specialists who devote themselves to some part of the agenda in government formation. Usually, the most salient and controversial matters – where bargaining relationships are divergent – are dealt with by party leaders themselves, as for example in Belgium, where party presidents have taken the lead in negotiating pacts on state reform (Timmermans, 1994). Müller and Strøm (2000: 574) report that agreements are made public in all countries except Luxembourg. By making their agreements public, parties increase commitments. The proliferation of public coalition agreements suggests that mistrust among parties has increased.

Size of coalition agreements   The size of coalition agreements varies enormously cross-nationally as well as within countries. In summarizing the findings on 13 countries, Müller and Strøm (2000: 575) report a variation between 200 words in Finland and over 43,000 words in Belgium. In most countries, the length varies over time with a factor 10, and also in most countries, the size of agreements has increased until the 1980s (see the country chapters in Müller and Strøm, 2000). On average, agreements are longest in the Netherlands (14,223 words) and Belgium (14,166 words). Both countries have a long experience with coalition government, but written coalition agreements did not exist until the late 1950s. As we saw, these two countries also have long formation processes involving different bargaining rounds, with multiple parties. But also countries where coalition government formation usually is less complicated have long agreements, as is the case in Norway and Portugal.

Contents of coalition agreements   More important than the length of texts formulated by coalition parties is what these texts have to say. Coalition agreements contain different kinds of intentions, varying between very general goals and specific policies and fine tuned instruments, and from vague intentions that nobody can reasonably disagree with to detailed compromises entailing substantive concessions. They may contain also other points of agreement such as procedures to be followed in decision making, competencies, and the distribution of offices within the new cabinet and at high political positions outside the cabinet.

In their comparative assessment, Müller and Strøm (2000: 576–578) have found that policies are the most central element in coalition agreements except in Italy, a country where coalition agreements are hardly in use. Also in Austria, arrangements other than policy intentions take up the largest part of agreements, but in the other countries, policies form usually over 90 percent of the commitments made between coalition parties. In Finland, France, Ireland, Norway and Sweden, coalition agreements are entirely or almost entirely devoted to policies (ibid.). What is interesting about the general or specific procedures incorporated in coalition agreements in most countries, is that these have become less prominent over time. Ostensibly, with the introduction of coalition agreements, parties felt a need to make rules of the game explicit. Parties may have internalized these rules and norms when participating in a coalition government – or at least they may have developed mutual expectations about this. More about these norms follows in the next chapter.

With the general increase in size of coalition agreements and the increased relative significance of policy intentions, also the scope of policy in agreements has broadened in most countries. In earlier times, parties building a coalition made informal agreements on a limited number of points that were not written down. When a new government took office, the prime minister simply gave a speech containing a general presentation of ambitions. This was for example the case in the Netherlands between 1945 and 1963 (Timmermans and Andeweg, 2000: 372). This explains why, in the analysis of Müller and Strøm, in a number of countries there are more cases of some form of agreement on policy (irrespective of their status) than coalition agreements (compare the tables on p. 574 and p. 582 in Müller and Strøm, 2000). As said, in most countries, written and published coalition agreements became part of coalition politics in the 1960s or later. In their quantitative analysis of coalition agreements, Strøm and Müller (2001) have found that the policy comprehensiveness of coalition agreements correlates most clearly to institutional rules within the cabinet. This is a set of variables for which it is more difficult to see why they are related to the contents of agreements than for example the variables pertaining to the bargaining context or to size and ideological properties of cabinets (but which appear to correlate much less strongly to the dependent variable). This finding from recent exploratory work on coalition agreements underlines that coalition research needs new theoretical directions. It suggests also that further exploration of empirical patterns of coalition behaviour is useful.

Chapter 3

Functions and Effects of Coalition Agreements

Policy negotiations between parties forming a government together are conducted to establish some form of agreement. Whether or not these negotiations are really substantive depends, among other things, on the extent to which the parties involved see differences in their respective preferences, the possibilities they see in government formation for dealing with these differences and, most fundamentally, the extent to which the parties are motivated by policy in the first place.

If variation in these points is possible, it is also possible that coalition agreements are perceived in different ways. What views on coalition agreements exist? What has the literature on coalition politics to say about this subject? In this chapter, I consider these questions. Informed by the comparative politics literature, possible functions of coalition agreements are identified, and this leads to another question: what are the empirical effects of coalition agreements? What difference do these written documents make to coalition politics? And if agreements may make a difference, what are the conditions on which particular effects may occur?

Ritual Dances or Real Chances: Two Views of Coalition Agreements

The recent exploratory work by Müller, Strøm and associates (2000, 2001, forthcoming) discussed in the previous chapter gives useful information on coalition agreements as the immediate output of government formation. This empirical attention is driven by the idea that coalition agreements are relevant. The existence of coalition agreements has been acknowledged in earlier coalition research, but this literature has contained rather diverse notions with respect to the meaning of these documents in coalition politics. Two different views of coalition agreements can be distilled from the literature.

Bargaining on Coalition Agreements as a Ritual Dance

The first view of coalition agreements, and of policy bargaining during government formation, is sceptical. Parties involved in government formation are seen to bargain on policy for a coalition agreement merely to underline their willingness to form a government together. They need to show to their followers that they do not just jump into office without asking a price from the other parties. Allegedly, their price is symbolical. Consider, for example, what Luebbert (1986: 52) has to say about this:

What makes the talks so long, difficult and complex is generally not the lack of goodwill among elites, but the fact that negotiations must appear the way they do in order to satisfy the members whose orientations are still largely attuned to the vocal, symbolic, and ideological aspects characteristic of each respective political subculture. It is wrong to assume that, because interparty negotiations take a long time, much is being negotiated among the parties. Most negotiation in cases of protracted government formation takes place between leaders and their followers and among rival factions within parties.

Luebbert sees parties as arenas of competition for leadership positions not less than as actors in competition with other parties. As the above citation illustrates, the author depicts party leaders primarily as policy users, less as policy seekers. In this view, coalition agreements, before anything else, are elaborated for intraparty purposes. It is also worth quoting what Laver and Schofield (1990: 189) say about coalition agreements:

While such a document is unambiguously the immediate output of coalition bargaining over policy, we must none the less be wary about its real political significance. It might, after all, be little more than window dressing.

Furthermore (1990: 191–92):

There are several reasons why it is difficult to read a meaning into what appears on the face of it to be a fairly straightforward document (...) For example, parties with fundamental policy disagreements that none the less decide to go into government together will not want to draw attention to what divides them. Conversely, when there is clear agreement between parties on policy, they are likely to publicize this, however trivial the issue (...) Thus the published policy statement is a highly strategic document, the meaning of which is obscure to all but the most sophisticated of insiders.

In a similar corner, Laver and Budge argue that published government programmes may not always reflect real government policy positions because they may be 'patched up hastily between party leaders more as a public relation exercise' (1992: 410; see also Klingemann, Hofferbert and Budge, 1994: 33). Also Laver and Shepsle (1990; 1994; 1996) display a sceptical view of coalition agreements in their portfolio allocation approach. According to these authors, the most credible statement about the future policies of a government is not the coalition agreement but the allocation of portfolios to ministrables whose policy preferences are known. In their view, ministerial autonomy is large, and more important than policy packages made between parties during government formation.

But is it true that, as Laver and Schofield assert, parties deciding to form a government together avoid drawing attention to major policy conflicts between them? Will these parties emphasize only the points of agreement on non-contentious or even trivial issues? Apart from the need for party leaders to temper their own office-seeking drive to avoid alienation from their party rank and files, there is the problem of manifest policy conflicts among the parties. If parties do not immediately draw attention to policy disagreement in public, such disagreement may still exist. Ignoring this during government formation may be a form of self-deception.

Bargaining on Coalition Agreements as a Real Chance

The second view of policy bargaining in government formation takes coalition agreements more seriously. In one of the earlier works on coalition governments, Browne and Dreijmanis (1982: 349–50) conclude for instance:

> The key process which determines the value of coalition membership is seen to be the negotiation of a more or less formal agreement or bargain specifying the general expectations which actors may have of one another as coalition partners. Most authors agree that the primary concern of actors during these negotiations is to achieve an agreement which commits the government as a whole to a set of policies as similar as possible to their own policy positions. (...) In addition to establishing programmatic content to guide the behavior of cabinet coalition members, negotiation of a coalition agreement also provides the partners with an opportunity to establish the extent of their influence over the process of policy determination.

Though the country chapters on which Browne and Dreijmanis base their conclusion contain little systematic evidence of a substantive role for coalition agreements during the lifetime of governments, the view they present is interesting.

The work of Peterson, De Ridder, Hobbs, and McClellan (1983) and Peterson and De Ridder (1986) is more directly focused on the role of coalition agreements. In contrast to the argument of policy avoidance during government formation, these authors call government formation a policy making arena par excellence. In their view, government formation is an 'institutionalized extrainstitutional arena' and it forms an important stage in a cumulative process of policy making. The government formation arena is seen to have the advantages of an informal context, with less constraining rules than in the legislative arena (ibid: 82; Peterson and De Ridder, 1986: 567).

One key aspect of this approach of government formation is that it not only is the start of a process of policy making in a particular coalition government, but also follows immediately after the end of the previous government. Issues that caused a government collapse often return on the agenda during the formation of a new government. Policy conflict is an important cause of government dissolution. Müller and Strøm (2000: 586) show that in typical coalition systems, interparty conflict is the second most frequent mechanism of cabinet termination. But parties do not only consider the most disruptive issues; the scope of policy bargaining is broader, a point suggested by the comprehensiveness of coalition agreements in countries such as Austria, Belgium and the Netherlands.

As Peterson et al (1983: 72) say, the process of policy negotiations contains moments of evaluation:

> As the agreement is negotiated the participants are faced on each issue with the continual threefold choice of accepting terms, discontinuing negotiations or trying to improve terms through further bargaining; and those actors who are not direct participants in the negotiations are faced with continuous tactical choices concerning their relationship with the direct participants.

Finally, Peterson et al. (1983: 74) have called coalition agreements reference documents for policy making during the term of the government. As such these documents are seen to form at least part of the governmental agenda. More specifically, the agreement may

> (1) indicate a range of alternative courses of action to be considered or specify a preferred alternative, (2) specify a framework to be filled in by the government at a later date, (3) indicate other procedures for reaching further agreement, (4) develop specific legislative proposals to be presented to the parliament or present some combination of the above.

In more recent work, other aspects of coalition agreements have been highlighted. Blondel and Müller-Rommel (1993: 9) for example argue that during the negotiations on an agreement areas of potential conflict are reduced and eliminated, which may smooth the path of the government. This may be less because harmony prevails than because the coalition agreement constrains the scope of government action. Budge and Keman (1990: 47) also argue that reaching agreement among parties is important because it reduces tensions and costs of internal negotiation and also averts the risk of conflict which may bring down the government. Finally, Strøm and Müller (2001) not only analyze the content of coalition agreements but also assume that these agreements have strategic and substantive functions in coalition politics – a point that they consider worth further exploration.

In short, in the alternative view of policy bargaining during government formation, coalition agreements have a substantive meaning. This meaning may be substantive in the sense that coalition agreements matter for policy decisions that the government is entitled to take. This may be by mentioning the content of these policies, or by stipulating procedures for dealing with issues.

The two views of policy bargaining and coalition agreements are contrasting, but they may both contain elements of truth about the reality of coalition formation. The point to appreciate is that there may be a wide rage of issues included in coalition agreements and in government programmes, but only a limited number may have been the object of real bargaining between parties. An empirical analysis of policy bargaining during government formation and the results incorporated into a coalition agreement should start with the identification of the really central issues.

Functions of Coalition Agreements

If drafting a coalition agreement is a ritual dance before parties allocate the seats at the cabinet table, there is little else to be said about this. But if parties see this process as a real chance to deal with policy, there may be more that drives them than only their interest in policy.

Reasons why Parties are Serious about Policy Bargaining

Other incentives for engaging in substantive bargaining are positive and negative. One possible reason that was mentioned briefly before is that policy conflicts may be inherited from the outgoing government, especially if the outgoing government broke down due to internal policy dispute. One or more parties of the outgoing government may be involved in the formation of a new government, and if this is the case, they may urge for attention to the contested issues before they may return on the cabinet agenda. This happens regularly in Belgium and Finland for example. Another point in the sphere of 'inheritances' concerns the political testaments drawn up by outgoing ministers and containing claims, often financial, in specific jurisdictions. The testament of the minister of Finance especially is considered to be important, particularly in periods of cutbacks in government expenditures.

A more general factor is the existence of mutual mistrust between parties. Of course, in competitive parliamentary systems, parties always display a certain level of mistrust towards each other. Mistrust in this sense is part of the game, and at least to an extent may be a matter of posture. Mutual mistrust however may also reach a higher level, beyond that stemming from electoral competition. Particular experiences may lead to increased mistrust; parties may also opt for strategies of polarization, which they may do to strengthen their electoral basis. Provided that mistrust does not hinder coalition formation in the first place, it may induce parties to give special attention to the coalition agreement. Comprehensive and specific coalition agreements may be regarded as an expression of this mistrust.

Apart from policy goals, previously experienced policy conflicts and mistrust between parties, another factor – in part reinforced by these relational points – is the institutionalization of government formation. In countries where the parliamentary groups of parties see government formation as an important venue for influencing coalition policy, expectations have accelerated the process of institutionalization. In these countries, coalition agreements have become so much a matter of course that it would take many by surprise if a new government took office without drafting such an agreement.

The combination of these different factors induces parties to make a serious job of drawing up a coalition agreement. This is important, as the institutionalization of government formation alone, for example, may explain why agreements have become longer and broader in scope, but the contents of arrangements – general or detailed – seems to depend more on the other factors. Mistrust, for example, may be an incentive for negotiating explicit and specific deals.

Symbols, Agendas, and Peace Keepers

Given the two views of coalition agreements and the incentives for taking policy bargaining seriously, three possible functions of coalition agreements may be distinguished (Timmermans, 1998). These are functions ascribed by the parties or party leaders themselves. They thus may be called the intended effects of coalition agreements, provided that coalition parties share these intentions during government formation.

Coalition agreements as symbolic gestures First, coalition agreements may have a symbolic function. They may be meant as such a gesture at interparty level, if leaders just want to emphasize their willingness to participate in the new government. This situation is the ritual dance. The agreement may also be a gesture at an intraparty level, and be used by party leaders to satisfy the party rank and file.

Party followers usually have certain expectations on particular policies, and these expectations are mostly a point of concern for party leaders, at least to the extent that meeting such expectations is necessary for re-election. When party leaders see policy negotiations in this way, coalition agreements will contain rather general intentions and goals that none will disagree with. Hence, once the new coalition government has taken office, a coalition agreement in such cases has the same value as a ticket after the cinema show.

Coalition agreements as policy agendas Following from the view of policy negotiations as a real chance and government formation as a policy making arena, parties may also ascribe more substantive functions to coalition agreements. Coalition agreements may be meant to predefine coalition policy. This may be called the agenda function. We saw that coalition agreements may be more or less comprehensive and more or less detailed, and this also is likely to be the case with different parts in these agreements. Some parts may contain substantive and specific intentions – cases of policy predetermination. Other parts of coalition agreements may contain general goals or mention which matters have to be dealt with in the coming years – cases of policy indication. This is a continuum, not a dichotomy, as in reality intentions included in coalition agreements may also take an intermediate form, without being really completely precooked decisions or only placing issues on the agenda. A measure of the degree of policy predetermination is the proportion of explicit compromises, containing clear commitments and doable intentions, relative to implicit compromises which are more vague and thus less committing.

Coalition agreements as conflict prevention devices Parties may attempt to predefine coalition policy not only because they take an interest in policy, but also because they want to smoothen the life of the government. They may try to prevent, as much as possible, controversial issues giving rise to political problems after the government has taken office. The third function, then, is the conflict prevention function.

The coalition agreement of the Eyskens IV government in Belgium, formulated in 1968, contained the following statement:

> This agreement exclusively regards those problems for which a basic agreement is indispensable. This enables the government to consider other possible problems in a calmer political climate (KHA, 1968: 419; author's translation).

Consider also this fragment taken from the coalition agreement of the Lubbers III government in the Netherlands, issued twenty years later, in 1989:

> Two large parties that want to form a new and cohesive coalition first must pay attention to agreements that bridge differences in viewpoints. Substantive and procedural arrangements form the point of departure of the government (TK, 1989–1990, 21132/8: 4; author's translation).

Coalition agreements may thus be meant to cement coalitions internally and streamline decision making within the government or the coalition at large. This may be either by listing procedures for dealing with particular controversial issues, or by piecing together substantive compromises. Here, the result also is a policy agenda which mentions intentions that must be implemented or elaborated during the government's term. At the same time, the parties may limit the scope of government action for the sake of peace and the continuity of the coalition. In that case, the coalition agreement may say that substantive decisions are postponed. Whatever the types of deals and phrases included in a coalition agreement, the document can have a conflict prevention function only if something is mentioned. Parties may have a explicit or implicit understanding that matters not included in the coalition agreement are also subject to norms of coalition discipline, but since deals and decisions on these issues need to be made during government life, the potential of conflict prevention is limited.

Coalition agreements may thus be formulated for different purposes, and for this reason they may have different functions for the parties involved. There is a certain hierarchy with regard to the three functions. This hierarchy represents the extent to which the agreement is believed to be instrumental to a substantive goal beyond government formation. At the lowest level, we find the symbolic function. If the agreement is meant to be merely symbolic, its purpose is to confirm that the parties are willing to form a government together. If the agreement is intended as a policy agenda, it may be instrumental to policy making by providing something between a general framework for policy making and a set of specific policies which can be implemented straight away. Finally, if the agreement is meant to prevent conflict on certain issues occurring or re-occurring within the coalition, it may warrant the continuity of the government coalition in office.

This conceptual hierarchy however does not mean that the three functions are mutually exclusive. If this is clear with respect to the agenda function and the conflict prevention function, it may also be the case with these substantive functions and the symbolic function. Even if parties see important points of conflict and engage in negotiations on these points, they may also devote paragraphs or even sections of coalition agreements to subjects on which everybody was happy from the start, and show the party rank and files that nothing has been forgotten.

Effects of Coalition Agreements

It is one thing to formulate a coalition agreement with substantive intentions. It is a different matter, however, to implement such intentions. As Finer noted: "When a government sets out to be 'faithful', it is frequently unwise, and when it has learned to be wise, it is frequently unfaithful." (quoted in Rose, 1984: 55). While Finer made this point in criticizing the 'manifesto moonshine' of single party governments in the United Kingdom, the elements of faith and wisdom may apply also to coalition agreements. The question is thus whether intended effects are also the actual effects of coalition agreements.

In this section, I deal with the possible empirical effects of coalition agreements. Not all parts in coalition agreements, however, may be relevant in this respect. As said in the previous section, parties may include a number of issues simply to meet expectations from followers or the general public without caring too much about these matters. In this section, the focus is on policy issues that are controversial during government formation. Often, such issues are key problems on the coalition formation agenda.

The results of bargaining on conflictual matters are explicit or implicit compromises, that is, arrangements containing substantive concessions or general and procedural agreements. To say that issues are conflictual however does not mean that hot issues always divide all parties – unless there are only two parties. In a three party coalition, for example, there may be conflict on three issues, none of which is disputed among all three parties. On each conflict, two coalition parties may be opposed to one other. Thus, policy conflicts may be more or less collective.

These points have important consequences for the way in which we see the possible effects of coalition agreements during the life of governments. Certain parts of coalition agreements may reflect perfectly convergent relationships among parties, or bargaining relationships that are tangential – issues varying in salience to the coalition partners. All 'doable' statements in coalition agreements may be elaborated and implemented, but the most interesting and significant matters for coalition politics are the ones the divide parties. On these issues, the inherent tension in coalition governments between 'togetherness' and party specific profiles is most clearly visible. While acknowledging that parties may not be able to write down intentions on really *all* points that divide them, what are the effects of deals and arrangements made on controversial policies?

Effects of Explicit and Implicit Compromises

Policy conflicts may take different forms, and the results of bargaining on conflictual issues may also vary. The distinction made by Luebbert between explicit and implicit compromises is relevant at this conceptual level. Explicit compromises were seen to contain unilateral or mutual concessions that are substantive and detailed. Implicit compromises were defined as agreements to disagree, which may consist of procedural arrangements such as postponements or statements which are sufficiently general or vague that none of the parties sees its preferences violated. Here, we may assume that implicit compromises emerge if central party values are at stake and issues do not involve quantities or are hard to define in such terms. These issues often will be in the fields of 'immaterial' policy: cultural, ethno-linguistic, and ethical questions. Explicit compromises are more likely to occur in the area of socio-economic policy, especially financial policy.

Following from the elements of policy and peace in the functions of coalition agreements, the effects of the two types of arrangements may be seen in terms of absence or recurrence of conflict among the parties and in terms of the implementation or nonimplementation of substantive or procedural arrangements. The four logically possible effects are thus (1) implementation of arrangements without conflict, (2) implementation involving conflict, (3) nonimplementation without conflict, and (4) nonimplementation involving conflict. The possibilities (3) and (4) may mean that decisions are taken in deviation from the agreement, or that no decisions are taken at all during the government's term in office. Given that the focus here is on issues that were controversial during coalition building on which some kind of arrangement was made, the least likely effect of any type of arrangement is (3), nonimplementation without conflict. Breaking a negotiated coalition commitment is unlikely to be accepted so easily by all parties; it will generate new conflict. Only in cases of early government termination (for some cause other than conflict over the arrangement in question) may this type of outcome occur. In such cases, one or more parties may end cooperation in the coalition also because they anticipate trouble on other issues and see more costs than benefits.

Explicit compromises may be seen as cases in which parties have engaged in policy predetermination, and to a relatively high degree of specificity. Parties will have invested time and energy in producing explicit compromises, and this may increase their commitment to implement such compromises. This type of arrangement may be expected to be functional both in terms of policy and in terms of peace. This leads to the hypothesis that explicit compromises have a type (1) effect: they are implemented without conflict.

Implicit compromises written down after bargaining on controversial policy are less doable, and they reflect less agreement – or even continued disagreement – among the coalition parties on what should be the contents of government policy. This may have induced these parties to satisfy themselves with a procedural arrangement in an attempt to avert further political trouble. In terms of policy, the effects of implicit compromises may become visible only after some time, if there are any substantive effects at all. Policy intentions in implicit compromises need elaboration, or policy problems are removed from the agenda either temporarily or for the entire term by some procedure. Given these possibilities, it is useful to distinguish between implicit compromises that have something but not much to say about the contents of policy, and implicit compromises with a procedural character. Such procedural arrangements can be considered to be really different from the other type of implicit compromise if they are doable – if it is stated clearly how the coalition parties should go about in decision making, what they should do and not do. While substantive implicit compromises may have a positive agenda function (they place issues on the government agenda), procedural implicit compromises are often meant to have a negative agenda function.

Expectations about the effects of these two types of implicit compromises may also differ. While substantive implicit compromises leave much or practically everything to be fleshed out by the government coalition, procedural implicit compromises are at least specific about the courses of action with respect to the issue. Procedures containing temporary postponements or clauses prohibiting parties to deal with the issue at all are often made specifically with the conflict prevention function in mind. This leads to the hypothesis that procedural implicit compromises have a type (1) effect: they are implemented without conflict. This is the same expected effect as explicit compromises, but an important difference is that implementation here concerns the agreed procedures, not substantive policy intentions. Implicit compromises with a substantive content are expected to be less functional to conflict prevention, and implementation in such cases involves interpretation and elaboration by the coalition partners. The hypothesis thus is that substantive implicit compromises have a type (2) or a type (4) effect: implementation involving conflict, or nonimplementation involving conflict. Compared to explicit compromises, the expected effect is that policy decisions result from substantive implicit compromises less often, and with more conflict. They boomerang interparty conflicts back into the coalition government.

The Problem of Enforcement

The different types of arrangements on policy thus may have different effects, and this raises the crucial question how coalition agreements are enforced. Coalition agreements are not legally binding contracts that are enforced by an external actor such as an independent judge. Even explicit compromises that are clear cut and doable can not be considered to be selfpolicing. As Hobbes (1968: 196) observed: 'For he that performeth first, has no assurance the other will performe after; because the bonds of words are too weak to bridle mens ambition, avarice, anger, and other Passions'. Enforcement of agreements is thus endogenous to the coalition and, as such, it is a part of the politics of coalition.

Parties in a government coalition have established cooperation, but they also have incentives – ideological and electoral – to maintain their own identities, and profile themselves *vis à vis* each other. Arrangements in coalition agreements will not often contain equal payoffs to all parties. Issue linkages may not always be possible because the decision making capacity of governments is limited. Particularly on matters of high politics, governments may need to shift from parallel to serial processing. If the relevant issues on which compromises were made in coalition formation are on the government agenda, parties may begin to look differently at these compromises – they may begin to feel the costs. Parties may engage in which Lax and Sebenius (1991) call 'process opportunism', and try to sabotage the implementation of points in the coalition agreement. Keeping all parties on the track set out during government formation then can become difficult. How, then, can coalition agreements be enforced during the term of the government?

Moral Obligation and the Norm of Reciprocity

Probably the most widespread notion about enforcement of coalition agreements is that they are morally binding: *pacta sunt servanda* (pacts must be observed). Bogdanor has called coalition agreements the constitution of coalitions. According to this author, the agreement must be honoured in good faith if the coalition partners are to maintain confidence in each other (1983: 271). The notion of moral obligation is even included in the text of coalition agreements. The first written coalition agreements in the Netherlands (1963 and 1965) started with a paragraph on what was called 'the nature and extent of commitments'. The agreement issued in 1963 for instance stated that:

> Beside the 'formal' commitment, there is also the moral commitment, which is in the nature of the agreement and exists between the government and the affiliated groups in parliament (Handelingen Tweede Kamer, Buitengewone Zitting, 1963: 122; author's translation).

If not explicitly mentioned in the text of agreements, this kind of commitment certainly was also felt in more recent coalitions. As one Dutch minister recalled in 1986:

> We promised to honour the coalition agreement. The only thing we really discussed in the government's constituent meeting was the value of the coalition agreement (...) We all felt that the agreement was not something to be forgotten so easily (...) Indeed, some ministers always had the document with them (Van Tijn and Van Weezel, 1986: 62–63; author's translation).

The principle of *pacta sunt servanda* is strengthened by the interdependent nature of obligations of the partners (Gilbert, 1993) and, as Hardin (1990) notes, on trust as 'encapsulated interest'. The norm of reciprocity is sustained by mutual control between coalition parties – defection is prevented by the prospect of similar action of others and by the need to maintain a reputation as a credible coalition partner in the future. As Hobbes (1968: 192) put it: 'Bonds, that have their strength, not from their own nature, (for nothing is more easily broken than a mans word,) but from Feare of some evill consequence upon the rupture'. The multi issue character of coalition agreements implies that reprisals are possible, and that each party weighs this threat against the expected benefits from defection. The risk however is that in this process one party uses the 'big gun', the threat to bring down the government.

Conditions for Enforcement

The norms for enforcing coalition agreements are what Scharpf (1997: 142) calls a weak institutional regime. This raises the question what other factors may play a part in enforcement.

Coalition size and reciprocal control The strength of reciprocal control may depend on coalition properties, such as the number of parties. The assumption is that as the number of coalition parties increases from two to three or more, reciprocal control becomes more difficult to maintain (becomes less effective). This may be so, even if during government formation policy conflicts do not always involve all parties. With three or four parties, the complexity of bargaining relationships may mean induce an individual party to call into question a particular compromise when the other parties are expected not agree so easily about how to respond. Perhaps, one of the other parties even supports the idea of renegotiating the arrangement. This may be the estimation of each individual party, and the result may be a gradual erosion of the coalition agreement as matters are placed on the cabinet agenda. This process may go on until to one party the price becomes too high, forcing a coalition crisis.

In two party coalitions, reciprocal control may be stronger. In face to face bargaining relationship of two parties, retaliation seems to be a more serious threat. Only an external party could give one party its support when challenging particular arrangements. This however is something to which the second party may react not only by making similar manoeuvres, but also by threatening with a coalition crisis. For this reason, an appetite for forming legislative coalitions with external parties may be reduced.

Briefly, in situations in which payoffs from coalition bargaining are distributed unequally at the level of individual arrangements but not at aggregate level, the mechanism of reciprocal control may be more effective in two party coalitions. The likely result is that in these coalitions the degree of implementation of arrangements, explicit and implicit compromises, is higher than in multi party coalitions.

Coalition governance arenas Coalition agreements are made during government formation in what Peterson et al. (1983) have called an 'institutionalized extrainstitutional arena'. The advantages of this setting are lost in part when matters arrive on the agenda in parliament and in the cabinet. For this reason, parties may want to create informal structures less exposed to the broader public and the media in which enforcement of coalition agreements can be organized. Coalition committees are one example of such informal arenas, of which the forms vary across countries (Andeweg and Timmermans, forthcoming). They contain spokespersons, and often prominent members, from different sections of the parties, and they may vary in size. The exact composition will vary from case to case, and depends, in part, on the internal power structures within parties. Coalition committees should further be distinguished from formal and informal cabinet committees and parliamentary committees, which are within the sphere of the cabinet and parliament.

If coalition committees are present, they may form an alternative arena of policy making and facilitate the resolution of conflict. This alternative arena may resemble the government formation arena, even if it is confined to particular policy fields. The assumption is that the presence of a coalition committee is a favourable condition for the implementation of coalition agreements.

Negotiators as ministers   At the level of the government, we may distinguish between ministers who have participated in policy bargaining and ministers without this background. If the 'founding fathers' of the coalition participate in the government and take portfolios in the fields of policy bargaining, arrangements may be elaborated and implemented more easily. This may be the case especially if these ministers form the top of the cabinet (the prime minister and one or more vice prime ministers, for example. Ministers who have not been a negotiator may see the coalition agreement as a package of *faits accomplis*, and even if they are willing to carry out arrangements, these arrangements may not always be entirely clear or perhaps contain elements of which only the negotiators are able to give a uniform interpretation. To ensure that ministers understand and/ or accept the arrangements in their field of jurisdiction will not be easy, especially if these ministers see their job as one involving policy making autonomy. The assumption therefore is that the presence of negotiators in the government facilitates enforcement of coalition agreements. If outsiders take the portfolios in fields of intense policy bargaining, this increases the likelihood of conflict and reduces the prospects of smooth implementation.

Prime ministers as coalition coordinators   In most countries, the *formateur* becomes the new prime minister. He or she may also have participated in policy negotiations. The prime minister is thus often an insider; but even without such involvement in government formation, the prime minister may have the special task of streamlining cabinet decision making. The prime minister may have agenda setting powers and be responsible for keeping the coalition together by arbitrating in conflicts. This implies a monitoring the role of the prime minister.

The extent to which the prime minister may have a positive, or negative, influence on enforcement of coalition agreements depends on competencies, on role perception, and on the perception of payoffs from arrangements. If the prime minister was involved in policy bargaining and finds the results satisfactory, he or she may guard implementation of explicit compromises and be a guide in elaborating implicit compromises. As an *activist*, the prime minister has more explicit political stakes in implementation, or in hindering implementation, than when acting as an *arbitrator*, a role focused on conflict resolution (Blondel and Müller-Rommel, 1993: 14–15).

Internal party unity   Parties are not always internally homogenous with respect to policy questions. During government formation, internal unity and discipline may still be preserved because the party's bargaining position is at stake. But once the new government is in office, internal unity may disappear. In countries where the internal rules of parties require that the results of formation bargaining are formally approved, usually at a party congress or a special delegates conference, internal party divisions may become manifest before the formal installation of the government. Institutionalized groups or factions led by party prominents may make the life of formal party leaders difficult. Internal divisions within parties manifesting themselves make enforcement more difficult; conversely, unified coalition parties increase the likelihood of implementation of coalition agreements.

Economics and personal chemistry   Two final factors that may influence enforcement are the state of the economy and personal relationships within the coalition. The economic situation may be most directly relevant to implementation of arrangements on financial/budgetary and socio-economic policy. Compromises made in these fields may come to be considered out of date by some or more parties.

Even if more structural conditions are favourable, stressed personal relationships can cause lots of trouble in coalition politics – thus also hamper enforcement of coalition agreements. The point here is however that personal chemistry most often manifests itself in negative cases; that is, personal clashes that destabilize coalitions are more visible, and are made more visible in accounts of politics, than cases of harmony.

These different factors relating to different aspects and different levels of coalition politics are likely to play a part in the process of enforcement of coalition agreements. No single factor is expected to be a sufficient or necessary condition for success. Moreover, the terms 'success' and 'failure' may mean different things to different parties. Here, they concern the question whether or not compromises and other types of arrangements in coalition agreements are implemented and/or prevent that interparty conflicts reoccur.

Further, in this book, implementation is confined to the political sphere; the analysis does not extend beyond formal approval of government acts – in whatever form – and thus does not deal with implementation of policies by agencies and street level bureaucrats. Thus, we may speak of success if arrangements (procedural or substantive) are carried out and, in the case of substantive arrangements, decisions are approved in the formal decision making institutions. For some decisions, government approval will be sufficient, but for others there may be the additional requirement of parliamentary approval, as in the case of legislation.

Summary and Conclusion

The existing variation in general features of coalition agreements across European countries is reflected in the notions on the meaning and functions of these documents. In one view, negotiations on coalition agreements are depicted as a ritual dance around the government formation table, the purpose of which is little else than demonstrating to the party rank and file and the outside world that a coalition is viable. In the other view, policy bargaining has a more substantive meaning, which carries beyond the installation of the government. Party spokespersons pay attention to policy before taking office because they care about policy. Other incentives are programmatic demands from within the parties and mistrust among parties. Parties may invest in the new coalition by removing conflicts as much as possible during government formation.

These views suggest three possible functions of coalition agreements. Party leaders may draw up an agreement for largely symbolic reasons; they may formulate common and general policy intentions merely as a confirmation of their cooperation in a new government coalition. But party spokespersons also may engage in policy negotiations to predefine coalition policy, especially on important and controversial issues. Parties setting out to do this see a coalition agreement as a coalition agenda containing substantive or procedural commitments to avoid that conflicts occur later on.

The effects of coalition agreements may vary. Focusing on matters on which parties direct most of their attention during government formation, the controversial issues, the effects may be seen in similar terms as the functions of agreements: policy implementation and conflict prevention. Explicit compromises, as substantive and relatively specific arrangements, are expected to be implemented without giving rise to new conflict. Procedural implicit compromises also are expected to be implemented without conflict, but the price for this is that no substantive policy decisions are taken. Substantive implicit compromises need further elaboration, and the expectation about this type of arrangement is that implementation involves conflict, and leads to substantive policy decisions less often than when explicit compromises were made.

These hypothesized effects of arrangements cannot be seen in isolation from favourable or unfavourable conditions for enforcement of coalition agreements. Even detailed compromises are not self-policing – some mechanism of enforcement is necessary. Favourable or unfavourable conditions for implementation of coalition agreements concern characteristics of the actors within coalitions and the arenas in which these actors meet. The broader economic environment is also likely to be relevant.

These conditions for enforcement must be understood as factors influencing the choices and behaviour of parties and party spokespersons such as ministers engaged with the implementation of the coalition agreement. The enforcement problem must be seen in the light of the continuous temptation for individual parties to try to increase payoffs from arrangements, but also in terms of uncertainty. Enforcement involves elements of faith and wisdom, and success and failure in implementing coalition agreements have a relative meaning. The conditions mentioned in this chapter may or may not appear to be important in real world cases of coalition governance. It is to these cases that we turn in the next chapters.

Chapter 4

Case Studies: Coalitions in Belgium and the Netherlands

How can the functions and effects of coalition agreements be studied empirically? The existing literature on coalition politics does not provide an answer, so it is necessary to consider this question here. This chapter introduces a case study approach to open what is still largely a block box of coalition politics: the different types of effects of coalition agreements, and the conditions on which these effects occur. The countries from which the case studies are taken from Belgium and the Netherlands, where coalition agreements are comprehensive. This chapter give a more extensive introduction to the politics of coalition agreements in Belgium and The Netherlands, and presents a case selection.

Turning Conflicts into Deals, and Putting Deals into Practice

Conflictual policy issues are the point of departure in the empirical study in this book. It is important to distinguish matters that are manifest conflicts during coalition formation from matters which are a potential source of dispute, but are not discussed. This second category of issues will not be considered. In the present context, manifest conflict means that parties conduct negotiations and try to hammer out an explicit or implicit compromise. As argued in chapter three, policy conflicts may become manifest in and after election campaigns, but they may also be inherited from the previous government, particularly if that government broke down over an internal policy dispute. Conflictual issues thus are input of government formation, and written arrangements on these issues are the output. As such, they are key elements of coalition agreements of which the effects will be assessed.

In the previous chapter, a number of expectations were given on the effects of explicit and implicit compromises. Do explicit compromises really prevent the recurrence of conflict and do they predelineate or even predetermine coalition policy? Are substantive implicit compromises counterproductive in terms of conflict prevention – concealing rather than resolving conflict? And to what extent are procedural implicit compromises effective mechanisms of procrastination? On the conditions for enforcement, what is the impact of coalition size, participation of negotiators in the government, and the other factors that may influence success or failure in implementing coalition agreements?

Coalition Agreements in Belgium and the Netherlands

Given the kind of questions to be dealt with, case studies of coalition government life are the most useful type of research. This is an exploratory study of functions and effects of coalition agreements, for which variation in cases is important. Cases of coalition government from the Netherlands and Belgium are selected on the basis of variation in coalition performance, that is, on the duration of governments and on their reputation in policy making, of which implementation of the coalition agreement is a part. The independent variable used in case selection is party composition, not only in terms of coalition size but also in terms of ideological profile. This variable is taken not with the intention to test a given theory but to see whether, in this exploratory study, party composition makes a difference. Thus, coalitions with different policy and survival performances and with different party compositions are analyzed. The case studies will be considered separately in the next chapters, but the emphasis in this book is not on comparing the cases as such. The aim of this study is to depict the empirical effects of coalition agreements in two countries where these agreements seem to be important, and introduce factors that may help explain why these effects occur – in these cases in Belgium and the Netherlands, but possibly also in other cases and countries with coalition agreements. As said, thus far, the empirical effects of coalition agreements and their possible explanations are a *terra incognita* in political science.

The two central countries in this study are the Netherlands and Belgium. One assertion – but still without systematic empirical evidence – about coalition agreements in the Netherlands is that they 'now have a fundamental influence on nearly all important decisions that a government must take' (Tops & Dittrich, 1992: 282). Coalition agreements also receive broad attention in the media. In both countries, there has been debate on the status of agreements and even on the supposed tension between the practice of formulating agreements and parliamentary democracy. In one view, coalition agreements have drastically reduced the role of parliament (Neels, 1975; Bovend'Eert, 1988). Clearly, these assertions are in need of empirical underpinning.

Low Country Coalition Politics

Belgium and the Netherlands are placed in the tradition of the politics of accommodation, but both systems became more polarized and politicized in the late 1960s (Dewinter, Timmermans and Dumont, 2000; Timmermans and Andeweg, 2000). The emergence of coalition agreements in the mid 1960s is an expression of politicization and the increase in mistrust among parties, but can also be seen in the tradition of accommodation – an element of continuity with somewhat different means.

Polarization and politicization have become manifest in different ways. At the level of the bargaining system, interparty hostilities have increased. In the Netherlands, the Social Democrats (PvdA) and the Liberals (VVD) have mutually excluded each other since 1959, and in 1967, the PvdA took a polarizing strategy and tried to form an alternative to governments including the Christian Democrats (CDA, a merger of three parties in 1980), which were in office continuously between 1918 and 1994. In Belgium, the traditional party 'families' split into separate French speaking and Dutch speaking parties in the period between 1968 and 1978, while in the same period, the regionalist parties (the Flemish People's Union, VU, the *Rassemblement Wallon*, RW, and the Democratic Front of Francophones, FDF, based in Brussels) became relevant in the coalition game. In the 1980s, the regionalist parties declined, especially the French speaking ones, and coalition politics increasingly came to be dominated by the Dutch speaking CVP and the Wallonian *Parti Socialiste* (PS), the two largest parties. In 1989, Belgium became a federal state, with separate party systems and governments.

In the 1970s, policy bargaining in government formation became truly multidimensional – parties had to deal with issues in several policy fields where preferences are conflicting or even contradicting. In Belgium, language and community issues appeared on the political agenda, and economic recession in the mid 1970s gave rise to interparty conflict on financial and economic matters on which both ideological and regional cleavages were playing a part. Though other matters do not appear to be permanently salient, subjects relating to the religious cleavage (school policy and ethical issues such as abortion) also emerged on the government formation agenda (De Ridder and Fraga, 1986: 386–388).

Financial and economic issues also formed and still form an important subject of interparty negotiations in the Netherlands. Other relevant matters in this country are policy on real estate, the media, nuclear policy, and, as in Belgium, issues relating to the religious-secular divide (Maas, 1982).

Processes and Products of Government Formation

Government formation in the Netherlands and Belgium is not always preceded by parliamentary elections. In both countries, *fliegende Wechsel* (coalition changes without elections) have occurred, and only in the Netherlands this practice was abandoned, in 1967. In Belgium, four different governments were formed on the basis of one election in 1980. Typically, in both countries, the decisiveness of parliamentary elections is low: relevant parties gaining seats often 'lose' in government formation, and parties suffering electoral defeat still become a government member – though the more recent dramatic election results in the Netherlands in 1994 and 2002 were hard to ignore, and were not ignored in coalition building. Pre-electoral coalitions are relatively rare. These points are indicators of government formation complexity.

Government formation consists of three stages, with policy negotiations often (but if not always) following after a party combination is formed. The distribution of portfolios is always the final stage (Peterson et al, 1983; Laver and Budge, 1992: 415). In both countries, however, the party configuration sometimes changes during the discussions on policy, so that the two stages may overlap. Belgian and Dutch coalition governments involve more aborted attempts than in other Western European countries, and they also take more time to be formed (Müller and Strøm, 2000: 570). The relationship with the emergence of coalition agreements however is not straightforward; long negotiations may result in brief coalition agreements, and sometimes extensive documents were produced in a relatively short time.

Initially, coalition agreements were put together by party leaders only. In the early 1970s, parliamentary specialists or other party spokespersons became involved. In the Netherlands, those participating in policy bargaining are usually parliamentary leaders and members of the parliamentary groups. In Belgium, the most prominent negotiators are the party presidents, accompanied by other party prominents or parliamentary specialists. In 1988, for example, not less than 15 top negotiators and 70 other party spokespersons were involved in Belgium (De Ridder, 1989: 186–187).

The form of the negotiations is usually determined by the *informateur*(s) or *formateur*(s), or in Belgium occasionally by a *mediateur*. If there are two or more formation attempts, there are often different ways of proceeding. Despite the fact that in the low countries government formation is institutionalized, both the procedure and style of the (in)formateur(s) varies considerably from one government formation to the other. Initially, conflictual issues were first identified and then dealt with sequentially. As the agenda became more substantive and the number of issues increased, matters came to be dealt with more synchronically. This was made possible by setting up work groups, each dealing with one particular part of the agenda. Government formation accounts mentioned such work groups for the first time in the Netherlands in 1971, and in Belgium in 1972. More recently, the use of work groups in the Netherlands is combined with what is called a concentric approach (1982, 1986, 1989) – party spokespersons begin by discussing general policy areas, and in following negotiation rounds they focus on the really wicked problems. This approach, but without work groups, was used also in the formation of the centre right three party government in 2002 in the Netherlands.

Whatever approach is followed, the most important matters are usually dealt with by party leaders themselves. These matters may be kept for the final round of negotiations, but sometimes they are dealt with first. In such cases, the issues are felt to be so important that reaching agreement is a condition for the viability of the coalition, and for continuing negotiations. This approach is followed particularly when a government broke down after policy dispute. For example, in 1965, public broadcasting triggered the fall of a government of Christian Democrats and Liberals in the Netherlands, and the issue was given priority during the next government formation.

In both countries, the proportion of ministers involved in the production of coalition agreements varies between one third and two thirds. In the Netherlands, parliamentary leaders often become a minister, though only in 1971 and 1981 was this the case within most parties that took office. Party presidents in Belgium have entered the government less often. There is thus variation in this condition for enforcement of coalition agreements.

The tendency towards more extensive and specific documents seems to be unrelated to any particular type of coalition or combination of parties. In 1963, the first coalition agreement in the Netherlands was, in the view of prime minister Marijnen, 'not a complete government programme' (Handelingen Tweede Kamer, 1963: 70), this changed in the 1970s. The first joint programme also called a coalition agreement was issued in 1971. In the early 1980s, coalition agreements became longer and more detailed. The average length of agreements in the 1960s was some 3,500 words, doubled to about 6,500 words in the 1970s and further increased to nearly 20,000 in the 1980s and to over 25,000 words in the 1990s (Timmermans and Andeweg, 2000: 374).

Belgian coalition agreements also became quite long in the same period: 4,500 words in the 1960s, 13,000 in the 1970s, 20,000 in the 1980s (Dewinter, Timmermans and Dumont, 2000: 331). In the 1990s however the average length of agreements dropped, and this is may be a result of federalization, rendering detailed compromises on language and state reform issues less necessary. As in the Netherlands, the first agreement, issued in 1965 and called the appendix to the government declaration, was 'not intended to be an extensive and detailed inventory of problems at the level of individual ministries' (Parlementaire Handelingen Kamer, 29 July 1965). Another similarity between the two countries is that the term coalition agreement was used first in 1972.

The practice of formulating comprehensive coalition agreements goes with an increased life of governments in Belgium and particularly in the Netherlands. But one other feature of both countries is that the most frequent cause of government termination is internal conflict (Timmermans and Andeweg, 2000: 387). These points seem contradicting, and thus it is necessary to consider more carefully the possible causality in the relationship between coalition agreements and government performance. This relationship between agreements and peace and survival is examined in detail in the case studies that will be introduced in the next section.

Selection and Design of Case Studies

As said, this exploration of the different possible effects of coalition agreements and conditions for enforcement requires variation between cases. The cases are taken from the period between the early 1960s, when coalition agreements first appeared, to the late 1990s. But since coalition agreements became comprehensive documents only in the early 1970s, the first decade of coalition agreements is not considered. The key point here is that case selection should lead to results that are not biased, for example by taking cases that all would be about short lived governments failing to implement the coalition agreement, or by analyzing only stories of success. This means that at least two governments per country must be analyzed, one that is really short lived and one that has lasted at least as long as the national average of government duration, and thus has had more time to implement intentions in the coalition agreement. In Belgium, average government duration is 1.4 years (Dewinter, Timmermans and Dumont, 2000: 343), and in the Netherlands it is 2.3 years, and even 3 years if caretaker governments are excluded (Timmermans and Andeweg, 2000: 387). Another selection criterion meant to create as much variation in this exploration as possible is party composition; coalitions consisting of different party combinations will be examined. As said, the assumption is that an increase in the number of coalition parties makes enforcement of the coalition agreement more difficult, and thus is likely to result in more conflict and less implementation.

On the basis of these points, five cases are selected. From Belgium, the Leburton five party government (1973–1974) consisting of the three traditional party families and lasting one year is analyzed, and the second Belgian case study deals with the Tindemans V five party government (1977–1978) composed of Christian Democrats, Socialists and two regionalist parties (Flemish People's Union, VU, and Democratic Front of French speakers, FDF), which lasted as long as the post-war average. For the Netherlands, the short lived Van Agt II three party government (1981–1982) including Christian Democrats, Social Democrats and Liberal Democrats is the first case. The Lubbers I two party government (1982–1986) formed by Christian Democrats and Liberals and lasting the entire constitutional term of four years is a second case. In addition, a third Dutch case included in this book is the more recent Kok I government (1994–1998), the first coalition since 1945 that excluded the Christian Democrats. This coalition thus was an innovation in terms of party composition, and it was rather heterogeneous in terms of socio-economic policy preferences.

Case Study Design and Key Concepts

Each case study contains an introduction of the coalition government and its context, an analysis of the policy conflicts during government formation and the deals included in the coalition agreement, and an analysis of the implementation of these deals. The relevance of conditions for enforcement – success and failure – is examined next.

The units of analysis in the case studies are the relevant parts of coalition agreements, that is, the explicit and implicit compromises made on policy conflicts during government formation. In one case, this may constitute only a limited part of the coalition agreement, and in another most of the document may cover this material. Coalition and government structures are the relevant context, which will be taken into account in each of the case studies when considering the impact of favourable or unfavourable conditions for enforcement.

Focusing on manifest interparty conflicts during government formation, on explicit and implicit compromises in coalition agreements, and on the degree of conflict prevention and implementation as effects requires that these concepts are well defined. The emphasis on *manifest* conflict during government formation is important, because only conflicts that are acknowledged and dealt with are considered. These are the point of departure in the analysis. In both countries, there is usually sufficient information about government formation to know what have been the central issues and conflicts during government formation.

Second, explicit compromises are, as said, those arrangements in coalition agreements that contain clear cut and doable substantive intentions. They are specific about what will be government policy. Substantive implicit compromises are much less specific, and for this reason they are less committing. Goals mentioned in this type of compromise are general or even vague, and instruments for reaching these goals are similarly vague or absent. Procedural implicit compromises contain no intentions about the substance of policy but state how the government and the coalition parties in parliament should deal with the issue. This may take the form of an agreement not to deal with the issue at all during the term in office, but it also may be some other procedure. The number of compromises obviously relates to the number of conflicts dealt with during government formation, but it is important to realize that the number of compromises may be larger than the number of contested issues. This is because during policy negotiations in government formation, a complex and contested issue may be decomposed to make agreement easier to reach. On one aspect, parties may compromise explicitly and on another point they may agree tot disagree and formulate some kind of procedure. Note also that the ways this is done can vary from one coalition to the other, and even from one policy field to another within one coalition. But compromises are always analyzed at the level of one issue, not at interissue level. Parties may and often do link issues during coalition bargaining, but what they agree on these issues is written down in separate parts of the coalition agreement. One reason to analyze the components of such larger policy packages separately is that when in office, parties often need to deal with them separately.

Third, the degree of conflict prevention and implementation of compromises are, in this book, indicators of the effects of coalition agreements (or at least the relevant parts), and as such they are coalition performance indicators. Success and failure are subjective concepts, but here they pertain to the prevention of conflict as one function of coalition agreements, and to policy implementation in relation to the agenda function – so irrespective of the evaluations of coalition costs and benefits that individual parties may make during coalition life. Thus, from its own perspective and given a particular strategic interest, one coalition party may consider implementation of a compromise (or even the nonoccurrence of conflict) a case of failure, and another coalition party may celebrate implementation. These dynamics may be manageable to some extent, but they are difficult to predict – a point that requires attention later in this book, after the case studies. In short, success and failure are considered at the level of the coalition at large, and the reference points are the compromises in the coalition agreement. Implementation of an explicit or a substantive implicit compromise is defined as a formal decision made and ratified in parliament or in (or on behalf of) the government. Though not all compromises may contain commitments to some kind of result (the commitment also may be that parties make an effort), a substantive formal result is used as the performance indicator in this analysis. Implementation of a procedural implicit compromise is defined as adherence to the procedure mentioned in the compromise. Conflict prevention is defined as the absence of new conflict on the issue during the life of the government. Relatively minor objections to a compromise made by a party (for example within the party organization, the parliamentary group or the party's team of ministers) but suppressed in one way or another are not considered new conflict. If internal party problems on a compromise lead to manifest interparty confrontation, this is seen as new conflict.

Chapter 5

The Leburton Government (1973–74)

Building a Five Party Coalition

In November 1972, the Eyskens V government of Christian Democrats and Socialists broke down on institutional reform, a subject prominent on the agenda since the revision of the Belgian constitution in December 1970. At stake was the forming of cultural groups and regions in Belgium. This was a political minefield impossible to survive for the Eyskens government, and after collapse the main parties realized that a new coalition government should have a sufficiently broad majority that institutional reforms could be guided safely through parliament. For some parts of these reforms, a two thirds majority was necessary. Since parliamentary elections were held only one year ago (November 1971), the building of such a broad coalition took place without new elections. The result was a coalition containing the three traditional party families: Christian Democrats, Socialists, and Liberals.

A new coalition controlling at least two thirds of the seats in parliament perhaps would be less vulnerable in institutional reform policy making, but by implication, the parties then should agree also in other fields of policy. And this was not automatically the case. None the less, interparty negotiations started with the subject of institutional reform and regionalization. Discussions first were between the two incumbent party families, the Christian Democrats (which had split into a Dutch speaking and a French speaking party in 1968, CVP and PSC) and the Socialists, BSP-PSB (still a unitary party but with two language sections). The focus of the *informateur* on institutional reform made the Socialists impatient: they demanded attention for socio-economic policy. The CVP and PSC put education policy on the formation agenda. On all these matters, the parties had divergent preferences. This became more pronounced when the two Liberal parties (PVV and PLP) joined the discussions, led by a *formateur*, the French speaking Socialist Edmond Leburton.

The policy scope of negotiations was broad. The key issues of regionalization and institutional reform were the rights for French speakers in the predominantly Dutch speaking Voer area on the language border which divides Belgium into a Dutch speaking part north) and a French speaking part (south), the elaboration of the new constitutional article *107 quater*, which entailed the forming of regions, and the tasks of the cultural councils, also newly formed bodies of which the jurisdictions still were unclear. Other controversial issues were economic policy, education policy, contraception and abortion.

On 19 January 1973, a coalition agreement was signed by the party presidents. Party support for the agreement however was far from unanimous, between and within the party families. The French speaking Christian Democrats had a 94 percent 'yes' vote, but the Dutch speaking CVP only a 60 percent majority. The

Liberals were equally divided, and the Socialist PSB-BSP showed a support of only 57 percent.

The coalition agreement had an unprecedented length of 21,000 words, and also was more comprehensive than before. It contained 18 different sections, in which intentions education policy, subsidies to the steel industry, allowances for war victims, institutional reform, energy policy, and morality issues were incorporated. CVP-president Wilfried Martens commented that 'the agreement contains ideological points which were not previously included in a coalition agreement'. His colleague of the Flemish Liberals stated that 'the ethical and moral issues are not just mentioned but are really matters on which the parties have made commitments' (De Standaard, 22 January 1973; Kamer van Volksvertegenwoordigers, 1973: 581).

The largest part of the document was on budgetary and socio-economic policy. During government formation, however, this field had received less attention than other issues. More time was spent on language policy, on which the previous government had collapsed. There was also a protocol mentioning procedures for decision making on several major issues.

The final stage of government formation was the distribution of portfolios. Since 1970, the Belgian constitution requires that cabinets are composed of an equal number of French speaking and Dutch speaking ministers, to principle of *language parity*. A large government ensued, containing 22 ministers and 14 state secretaries.[1] On 26 January 1973, after two months of negotiations, the Leburton government took office, and a few days later the parliamentary investiture was held.

Despite the ostensible investments made by the parties, some party spokespersons said that it was the vagueness of the arrangements made on contested issues that had led their party conferences to accept the coalition agreement. They said they were not very optimistic about the chances of government survival (De Standaard, 27 and 29 December 1972).

Turning Policy Conflicts into Deals

What were the contested issues during coalition formation? As said, a number of problems were inherited from the previous government, which had broken down on the issues of facilities for French speakers in the area of Voeren (Fourons) on the Flemish side of the language border, the competence of the cultural councils representing the communities of French speakers and Dutch speakers, and the forming of separate regions on the basis of article *107 quater* of the constitution. The delimitation of the boundaries of Brussels, which was to become the third region next to Flanders and Wallonia, was a source of intense conflict between the French speaking and Dutch speaking parties. These matters could not be ignored by a government formed to carry through institutional reforms. A conflict in a different field was on the position of religious schools, which divided Catholics and Socialists. Next, the issues of contraception and abortion were raised by the Liberals, who had high expectations from a coalition where the secular parties (Liberals and Socialists) were in a majority position. Finally, the parties dealt with items of socio-economic policy, but these received less attention than the other issues.

Language Policy

Disagreement existed on the granting of facilities, particularly educational, to the French speaking minority in the area of the Voer. This small area in the north east of the country consisted of six predominantly Dutch speaking municipalities in Flanders, containing a French speaking minority. These municipalities belonged to the Wallonian province of Liège, but in 1962 they were transferred to Flanders. Many residents in the Voer area however were oriented to the province and the city of Liège, and they had always violently opposed the transfer. The reverse situation existed in an area in the west of the country. The problem of the two areas on the language border, with most emphasis on the Voer area, had been on the agenda of successive governments, and also had contributed to coalition collapse.

The parties made an explicit compromise on the issue. It contained the granting of limited educational facilities to the language minorities in both areas, and the conditions for setting up schools also were relaxed. The parties expected that by formulating this compromise they had settled the dispute, so that they could concentrate further on regionalization and community policy (Luykx, 1973: 591).

A second issue was language parity in the administration of Brussels. A law of August 1963 stated that after 10 years (so by August 1973), language parity should exist at the top of the administrations of the 19 officially bilingual municipalities of Brussels. This provision always had been contested by the French speaking parties. Because the parity principle benefited the Dutch speakers, CVP and PVV referred to this law during government formation. In the coalition agreement, it was stated that the government would be competent to take special measures to ensure that language parity would indeed be realized by 1 September 1973. This was an explicit compromise with a zero sum character benefiting the Dutch speaking parties.

Regionalization Policy

In the constitutional revision of 1970, article *107 quater* stated that there would be three regions in Belgium: Flanders, Wallonia and Brussels. The two previous governments had foundered on the specification of the different articles of the constitution, which were often compromises. More specifically, points of conflict were the composition of representative bodies for the regions, the distribution of state subsidies between the regions, and the status of Brussels as the country's capital and official third region.

Regional bodies   The CVP advocated cultural autonomy for Flanders, which in the view of this party meant that the Flemish community and region should be one entity. This required a revision of the constitution. The other parties, particularly the French speaking ones, preferred that there should be separate representative bodies for the regions and communities. In the negotiations the CVP conceded on this point, the result being a postponement of the matter until after the term of the government (De Standaard, 5 January 1973).

The other points of discussion concerned the fleshing out of several constitutional articles. First, the parties agreed on a procedural arrangement mentioning deadlines for the submission of a bill by the government. A special parliamentary committee would examine the different articles of the bill. This committee was to be set up immediately and was to report before 15 July 1973 (six months after the government took office). To ensure the existence of a link between parliament and the executive, ministers, who in Belgium have a seat in parliament, were expected to participate in the meetings of the committee. If the committee did not come up with substantive changes or counterproposals, the government bill would be submitted officially in parliament. This was to be before 15 October 1973. In that case, the parliamentary groups of the coalition parties were supposed to be loyal and vote for the bill.

More substantive intentions were included in what was called the 'Scheme for implementation of article *107 quater* of the constitution'. This scheme contained the key elements for the bill referred to above and was binding, unless the coalition parties decided unanimously to modify it. The distinction made between a transitional and a definitive arrangement on representative and executive bodies was important. In the transitional stage, the regional councils of Flanders and Wallonia were to be composed of 60 members, to be recruited from the provincial councils on the basis of proportional representation. The Brussels regional council was to be composed temporarily of the provincial councillors residing in the Brussels agglomeration. These arrangements were to last until the first parliamentary elections after 1 January 1977, the elections following after the end of the constitutional term in office of the government. These points formed an explicit compromise.

In the definitive arrangement, which was to be enforced after the next scheduled elections in 1977, the regional councils would be composed of the provincial representatives with a reduction in the size of the provincial councils. The Brussels regional council was to adopt the functions of the existing Brussels agglomeration council. These points together also formed an explicit compromise. The commitments on Brussels entailed important concessions from the PSC, the party which was relatively strongly oriented on Brussels.

Next, another explicit compromise incorporated in the scheme for the implementation of article *107 quater* was that the executive bodies (regional governments) of Flanders and Wallonia would be composed of 9 members, who were to be elected from within the regional councils on the basis of the simple majority system. Each province within the region was to be represented in this executive body. The Brussels executive body was to contain 5 members, two elected by the Dutch language group in the Brussels regional council, two by the French language group, and the chairman elected by the regional council as a whole (as the majority was French speaking, this seat was likely to be obtained by someone from this group, though this was not stated explicitly). The arrangements for the three executive bodies were intended to be permanent; no distinction between transitional and definitive arrangements was made. The compromise entailed important concessions from the PSC and PLP (the parties with relatively strong electoral interests in Brussels), as these parties had demanded a two thirds majority of French speakers in the Brussels executive. It was still a compromise, because the Dutch speaking parties had demanded complete language parity (De Standaard, 10 and 15 January 1973).[2] The agreement also contained an escape clause to apply in case political problems would occur. It stated that if the forming of the Brussels regional council, and thus of the language groups which were to be its constituent parts, were impossible for political reasons, the Brussels executive would be elected by the French speaking and Dutch speaking groups of the existing Brussels agglomeration council.

Regional finance Another point of conflict was the distribution of financial resources provided by the central government to the three regions. The specific point of contention was the set of distribution criteria. If population size was taken as the main criterion, Flanders would take the biggest share, whereas the criterion of area size would benefit Wallonia, the larger region.

An explicit compromise was made, which stated that one third of the subsidies would be related to population size, one third to area size, and one third to the average revenues from income tax in the last three years. These criteria were to be included in the bill on regionalization (see above). This set of criteria, however, would be used only after three years, when the regional bodies took on a more permanent character. For the short term an explicit compromise was made, containing a distribution 50 percent for Flanders, 40 percent for Wallonia, and 10 percent for Brussels.

Brussels: problems of territory The third and most complex problem was delineating the boundaries of Brussels as the third region. Here, the lines of conflict also cut across the three traditional party families, and more between French and Dutch speakers than between Flamingants and Wallonians. Brussels is a largely French speaking city located within the Flemish region. The expansion of Brussels therefore implied a greater influence of French speakers in Flanders. In the perception of the French speaking Brusselers, there was a Flemish *carcan* (iron collar) around the city which hindered its expansion beyond the 19 municipalities which thus far constituted the capital city Brussels. To the Flemish, Brussels was a threatening oil stain which should be contained.

A procedural implicit compromise was made in which the issue was referred to the special parliamentary committee (which as said was to report to the government before 15 July 1973). The parties also formulated a kind of insurance arrangement, which stipulated that if the parliamentary committee was unable to agree, the Brussels region would coincide with the existing boundaries of the agglomeration (the capital city of Brussels). This arrangement was a major concession from the PSC and PLP.

Next, the Dutch speaking parties advocated the splitting up of the single Brussels electoral district into two separate districts. This would strengthen the electoral basis of the Dutch speaking candidates, and conversely reduce the influence of the French speakers. This was the reason why the French speaking parties (in particular the PSC) rejected this suggestion. The parties made a substantive but implicit compromise on this point, stating that a district division would be considered only as part of a general electoral reform. The government would submit a bill 'to simplify and harmonize the different electoral laws'.

Education Policy

Education policy traditionally divided Catholics and the secular parties. In the 1950s, state subsidies for private religious schools were high on the political agenda. After two successive governments, one a CVP-PSC single party government and the next a coalition of Socialists and Liberals, had pursued rather different policies in this area, a *National School Pact* was signed by the three traditional party families in 1958. The pact contained the official recognition of private next to public schools, including a system of subsidies for both types of schools. It increasingly became clear however that the school pact had not entirely resolved conflict, as the Catholics increasingly felt that private schools did not obtain sufficient financial resources, and were discriminated in this respect. For this reason, the CVP-PSC again placed education policy on the agenda.

Negotiations were to lead to a revision of the school pact, to be prepared by a new *National School Pact Committee*. This committee was to be composed of ministers, members of the parliamentary groups, and the presidents of the traditional parties. As such, it was a committee which cut across the boundaries of the formal decision making bodies. The CVP and PSC demanded that the school pact of 1958 be stretched up as much as possible, while the Socialists advocated minimal changes.

The parties made arrangements on these points, most of them explicit compromises. First, it was agreed that wages of clerical teachers would be increased. The CVP had demanded the abolishment of all (perceived) discriminations of clerical teachers compared with teachers at lay schools. The compromise stipulated that wages of clerical teachers 'not living in a religious community' would be increased to a level equal to the wages of officially licensed teachers. For those living in a religious community, a term which was left unspecified in the text, and teaching at primary or nursery schools, wages were fixed at 60 percent, and would increase to 70 percent of the normal wage after 15 years of duty. With regard to secondary schools, the school pact provisions of 1958 remained valid, which meant that clerical teachers would obtain the minimum wage, with an increase of 15 percent after 15 years.

Next, arrangements were made with regard to the size of different funds for public and private school construction and modernisation. A general plan on school construction was to be elaborated within six months by the government. The contents of this plan were left open. The size of a new general fund for school construction also was left undecided. Both arrangements were thus implicit compromises. More clear commitments were made on a fund benefiting public schools, which would consist of annual grants of 3 billion Bfrs., to be supplied by the national government over a period of ten years. A procedural arrangement on financial resources in the long run stated that the *National School Pact Committee* was to make a so called 'technical study' of the funds required on a long term, the results of which were to be presented before 30 June 1973. Further, a fund would be set up for annual credits for private schools. The CVP and PSC had demanded 5 billion Bf. per year, but the result of negotiations was an implicit compromise in which a largely symbolic amount of 180 million was mentioned, to 'underline that the parties have committed themselves' to create a real fund for private schools. On this matter too, the School Pact Committee was to elaborate the coalition agreement before 30 June 1973. Finally, there was an explicit compromise on the conditions for repayment of loans contracted by private schools. Such loans were to be repaid within forty years, and the interest rate would be that of the capital market reduced by 1.25 percent.

Socio-economic Policy

Though during the negotiations priority was given to regionalization and education policy, manifest differences on socio-economic policy could not be ignored. First, the parties disagreed on pensions for the coming years. The Liberals demanded a general increase in pensions, but the Socialists opposed such an increase if other sources of incomes, especially social benefits, were not increased as well. An explicit compromise was made on the issue, which stipulated that after a transitional period of three years, pensions (of employees) would become 75 percent for families or 60 percent for singles of the average wage in the private sector. Pensions for the self employed would be increased each year, to begin in January 1973.

Another issue was state intervention in the economy, in particular in industry. In the previous government, state activities had expanded, something opposed by the Liberals, who demanded a limited role of the central government in this field. Once at the bargaining table, the PVV and PLP asked for clarification about rumours of a secret agreement between the PSB and the Iranian state oil company (NIOC) on a large oil refinery project in the province of Liège, a troubled industrial area. The central question was whether or not the outgoing government had committed itself on this issue, something which in the eyes of the Liberals violated the conventional norm that controversial decisions are not taken when a government has caretaker status. The parties agreed implicitly on the issue. In the coalition agreement, it was stated that the government would be selective in initiating or stimulating economic activities, and would focus on those specific industries where initiatives by the private sector were staying behind. Such industries were to become public organizations. With regard to the oil refinery project, the agreement said that the government would await the results of the study.

Morality Policy: Contraception and Abortion

Two final controversial matters were the morality issues of contraception and abortion. Both issues were placed on the agenda by the Liberals, with support from the Socialists. With regard to contraception, the negotiators of the CVP and PSC were prepared to concede. An explicit compromise was made, which announced that the government would issue legislation to provide free contraceptives. This legislation was to be approved before the government reached the end of its term in office.

On abortion, however, agreement appeared more difficult to achieve. Abortion was prohibited, with the two Catholic parties preferring a maintenance of the status quo. Socialists and Liberals on the other hand strongly advocated a more liberal policy on abortion, not within the sphere of criminal law. The parties only agreed implicitly on the issue. Existing legislation on abortion would be revised before the end of the government, but the way in which this was to be done was left open. Table 5.1 gives the compromises made in different policy fields.

Table 5.1　Arrangements in Leburton coalition agreement

	Type of arrangement			
	explicit compromise	procedural impl. comp.	substantive impl. comp.	Total
Policy Field				
language	2	–	–	2
regionalization	7	3	1	11
socio-economic	1	–	1	2
education	3	1	3	7
morality	1	–	1	2
	14	4	6	24

Putting Deals into Practice

The expectation was that explicit compromises streamline government policy making more than substantive implicit compromises, and that procedural implicit compromises are primarily effective in terms of conflict prevention. What was the result during the term of the Leburton government?

Socio-economic Policy

The explicit compromise on pension policy was implemented without problems. A bill containing an increase in pensions of employees by 8 percent and, for subsequent years, the linkage of pensions to the economic trend was submitted to parliament and approved in March 1973 (Luykx, 1973: 596). A bill on pensions for the self employed was also submitted in parliament and approved without delay. The first responsible minister (a Liberal) declared that he was 'proud to have realized the intentions in the coalition agreement' (De Standaard, 24/25 March, and 16/17 June 1973).

A 'terminal' event: the IBRAMCO project　On state intervention in industry the parties had formulated only rather general intentions. The agreement stated that on the oil refinery project near Liège no decisions would be taken until a study on the profitability of the refinery was made. The Liberals even were assured that no further steps had been taken by the government. Shortly after the government had taken office, it however became clear that, during the term of the previous government, the Socialist PSB-BSP and the National Iranian Oil Company (NIOC) had started preparations for building an oil refinery in the province of Liège (Wallonia), under the name IBRAMCO (Iranian Belgian Refining and Marketing Company). Within IBRAMCO, the PSB-BSP controlled the Belgian seats on the board of directors.

The relevant paragraph in the coalition agreement was discussed at length within the government and in parliament. In May 1973, a motion was adopted in the Chamber of Representatives, stating that the government was committed to the agreement and was to communicate its course of action before 12 June 1973 (KHA, 1973: 321–322). On that date, the government did indeed make a statement on the issue, but it refused to go into the most delicate points. In October, prime minister Leburton emphasized that no decision would be taken before the study on the economic prospects of the project was done (KHA, 1973: 704).

At the same time, the consequences of the first oil crisis began to be felt in Belgium. In the view of the Socialists, the decline of heavy industry (steel) in Wallonia was an argument for building the refinery. The problem however was that Belgium was not the only candidate, and this was a reason for the NIOC to set a deadline of 15 January 1974. The CVP and PVV and PLP maintained their reservations against the project. On 16 January, one day after the deadline had passed, a compromise was reached within the cabinet. The NIOC however withdrew from the project, and when this withdrawal was confirmed, the ministers of the PSB-BSP resigned. On 19 January 1974, the prime minister tendered the resignation of the government (KHA, 1974: 56–57). The Leburton government had lasted one year, and this early end had its consequences for implementation of other parts of the coalition agreement.

Education Policy

On 28 February 1973, a protocol committing the parties to revise the school pact was signed by the *National School Pact Committee*. The committee was divided into four work groups which should report on 20 June 1973 (De Standaard, 1 and 27 March, 10 May 1973; Luykx, 1973: 601).

Religious communities In June 1973, conflict broke out within the government on the interpretation of the phrase 'clerical teachers living in a community', which was left unspecified in the coalition agreement. In the view of the Socialists, a religious community consisted of 3 members, but the CVP and PSC argued that the minimum was 9 members, which would mean that a smaller group of teachers would be brought under the special wage regime for clerical teachers, and receive only a certain percentage of the wages of lay teachers in public schools. Agreement could only be reached after painstaking negotiations. The government fixed the size of religious communities at 6 members; the difference was thus split (De Standaard, 7–27 June 1973).

School funds: who gets what, how and when? Conflict also resurfaced when the different implicit compromises on school funds were elaborated by the government. According to the PVV, the state school fund (3 billion Bf. annually) was to be used only for modernizing existing state schools. For the construction of new state schools, the general fund for school construction of public and private schools was to be used. This interpretation meant that claims on the general fund would increase. CVP-president Martens rejected this interpretation, as in his view the consequence was that less financial resources would remain for the construction and modernization of religious schools.

Preferences also differed about the size of the other funds. New substantive compromises were reached after extensive negotiations within the School Pact Committee as well as within the government. First, the fund for private schools was set at 3 billion Bf. a year. The conditions for credit remained those mentioned in the coalition agreement. This fund and the general fund for school construction would be placed under supervision of a special ministerial committee presided over by vice prime minister Leo Tindemans (CVP) until the end of 1973.

Meanwhile, the School Pact Committee was to carry on which the elaboration of a general plan, on which the parties had only committed themselves to conclude discussions by July 1973. This was postponed until 1 January 1974, and if on that date the plan still would not be completed, all funds would be blocked until the plan was presented (De Standaard, 27 June 1973; Luykx, 1973: 602–603).

These points were all elements of a new bill, which was approved in parliament in early July 1973. Only the general school plan continued to divide the parties, which led to another postponement until 31 March 1974 (De Standaard, 12 December 1973). Discussions on the plan were suspended when the government broke down in January 1974. Still, in this field, much of what was written in the coalition agreement was implemented within the year that the government was in office. Conflict however was not prevented.

Language Policy

The expectation that the compromise on the Voer and Comines enclaves was doable turned out to be largely correct. In the spring of 1973, the points mentioned in the compromise were implemented, and in early May, a new government decree on this matter took effect (KHA, 1973: 571).

In April 1973, the government submitted a bill in parliament containing special competencies for the minister of Internal Affairs to accomplish language parity in each of the 19 officially bilingual municipalities of Brussels (in most of these municipalities, the majority of the population was French speaking). Though the PSC and PLP had great difficulty with this bill (as with any policy based on the parity principle applied in Brussels), the bill none the less was approved in parliament in June, and language parity was established (De Standaard, 25 and 28/ 29 April 1973; 1973: 605–606). Thus, on these issues, the coalition agreement functioned as a policy predefinition and conflict prevention mechanism.

Regionalization Policy

What was the effect of arrangements on regionalization, given that the government lasted only one year? A point to be realized here is that what we consider in retrospective was not all foreseen by the parties. Even if the premature end of the coalition was related to developments in other policy fields as well, the end of the coalition was anticipated only shortly before the actual breakdown. Another point to appreciate is that several intentions had a shorter time horizon, such as the procedural arrangements mentioning deadlines (July, September, and October 1973).

Regional bodies   The coalition agreement committed the parties to refrain from initiating a constitutional revision. This commitment was observed, as no proposals were made. Another procedural arrangement which was carried out was the setting up of a special parliamentary committee on regionalization, in which members of the parliamentary groups took a seat. Spokespersons from the Democratic Front of Francophones (FDF) and the Walloon Rally (RW) were also invited to be present, but with no active role.

The committee had four months to advise the government on what the coalition agreement called the 'Scheme for the implementation of article *107 quater'* – the deadline being 15 July 1973. Despite the frequent meetings of the committee, no agreement could be reached on an alternative for the scheme mentioned in the coalition agreement (Luykx, 1978: 650).

Thus, the government faced the task of translating the points mentioned in the regionalization scheme into bills. This, of course, implied that there should be agreement within the coalition also on the points that were left unspecified during government formation. In July, a conflict broke out on the composition of the regional councils for what was called the 'definitive stage of regionalization' (this stage would begin after the scheduled parliamentary elections in 1977). The consequence of this conflict was that little progress was made with drafting legislation, which according to the coalition agreement was to be ready by mid October 1973. In October and November, several proposals were made and discussed, but differences between the parties could not be bridged (Luykx, 1978: 650; KHA, 1973: 703–704).

Discussions on the regional executive bodies also involved conflict, despite the explicit compromises which had been made on them. The composition of the Brussels executive especially divided the parties. This was a consequence of the earlier conflict on the Brussels regional *council* (De Standaard, 12 December 1973; Luykx, 1978: 650).

At the end of the year, the government gave 15 January 1974 as the new date for the submission of the bill on regionalization (the coalition agreement mentioned October 1973). Due to lasting conflict, even another postponement was necessary, and the end of the government meant that the issue had to be shelved until the formation of a new government.

Regional finance   A similar story can be told about regional finance. In October 1973, prime minister Leburton still stated that the government would observe the coalition agreement on the distribution ratio for financial resources provided by the central government (KHA, 1973: 704). When the arrangement finally was to be turned into legislation, however, the PSB and the PSC and PLP began to question the weighing of criteria mentioned in the compromise. Things were still undecided when the government terminated.

Boundaries of Brussels   The Brussels problem not only comprised political institutions but first of all the delineating of the boundaries of the Brussels region. If these were new problems, the problem of language already existed since the 1960s. The parties had made several arrangements during government formation on these matters, mostly implicit substantive compromises.

The special parliamentary committee working on regionalization was unable to find a solution to the geographical aspects of the Brussels problem. This meant that the status quo (Brussels boundaries coinciding with the agglomeration of 19 municipalities) would be maintained. The PSC and PLP however were no longer willing to support this arrangement, and the consequence was a deadlock within the government. On the issue of the Brussels electoral district, agreement also was to be re-established by the parties engaging in the formation of a new government.

Contraception and Abortion

With regard to contraception, the coalition agreement stated that the government would draft legislation in which the supply of contraceptives would be liberalized. In June 1973, such a bill was drafted by the cabinet committee on ethical problems. The bill was approved in parliament just before the summer break (De Standaard, 29 June and 6 July). Thus, the explicit compromise in the coalition agreement on this issue was carried out without giving rise to new political problems.

Things were different with respect to abortion, which was placed on the agenda but was further left undecided. In February 1973, the presidents of the CVP and PSC declared that their parties would accept abortion only on strictly defined medical grounds (De Standaard, 1 March 1973). Somewhat later, the Liberal minister of Justice completed a draft bill, in which abortion was allowed on several strict conditions. This bill was discussed in the ministerial committee for ethical problems, and would be submitted in parliament only if all coalition parties really agreed (De Standaard, 23/24 June and 5 July 1973). When the draft was discussed, the Socialists objected that the bill contained too many restrictions, and they decided to introduce a private member's bill. This bill however received little support from the Liberals (De Standaard, 8, 14 and 19 November 1973). The premature end of the government prevented that any further legislative action was undertaken.

Effects of the Coalition Agreement

Table 5.2 gives the effects of the relevant parts of the coalition agreement in terms of conflict prevention and implementation. The coalition agreement clearly was more functional in terms of policy delineation than in terms of conflict prevention (12 cases against 8 cases). But despite conflict, intentions mentioned in the coalition agreement were implemented – conflict thus did not mean policy deadlock in all instances. Policy delineation was not always policy predetermination. Sometimes, an issue was only placed on the coalition agenda, and substantive policy decisions followed only after further negotiations had taken place within the government or elsewhere. Other arrangements contained no substantive intentions but rather procedures for dealing with issues, or for *not* dealing with issues during the term in office of the Leburton government.

Table 5.2   Effects of Leburton coalition agreement

		Implementation		Total
		+	−	
Conflict prevention	+	6	2	8
	−	6	10	16
		12	12	24

Beyond these general observations, a number of expectations about the more specific effect of the three types of compromises exist. Explicit compromises, substantive and procedural implicit compromises were expected to have different effects. To what extent did these effects occur during the one year in office of the Leburton government? Have explicit compromises, as arrangements with clear cut and doable intentions, streamlined policy making? How much conflict resurfaced when substantive implicit compromises were elaborated? And have procedural implicit compromises prevented conflict and did they defer policy decisions? Table 5.3 presents the effects of the three types of arrangements, and also indicates in which fields these effects occurred.
lan = language policyedu = education policy

Table 5.3   Effects of types of arrangements

	Type of arrangement			Total
	explicit	procedural	implicit	
Effect				
implemented no conflict	4 (lan, so-ec, mor)	2 (reg)	−	6
not implemented no conflict	2 (reg)	−	−	2
implemented conflict	3 (edu)	1 (edu)	2 (edu)	6
not implemented conflict	5 (edu)	1 (reg)	4 (all)	10
	14	4	6	24

lan = language policy   edu = education policy   mor = morality policy
reg = regionalization policy   so-ec = socio-economic policy

The Streamlining Effect of Explicit Compromises

The expected effect of explicit compromises was that they are implemented without conflict. As table 5.3 shows, the actual effects of this type of compromise were different in most instances. Only the intention to establish language parity in the higher echelons of the Brussels administration and the compromise on facilities for language minorities on the language border, the arrangement on pensions, and the liberalization of legislation on contraception were implemented peacefully.

Three explicit compromises gave rise to inter-party conflict but nonetheless were implemented, an outcome which was typical of arrangements on education policy. The result was the submission of a bill on education policy and its subsequent approval in parliament, just before the summer break at the end of June 1973.

This contrasts with the effects of the five explicit compromises on regionalization, which generated rather than prevented conflict, and also were not implemented. Particularly the Brussels issue was a permanent source of conflict among the coalition parties; they were opportunistic in referring to the coalition agreement.

Finally, two explicit compromises on regionalization were neither a source of new conflict nor implemented. Intentions on the regional councils in the transitional stage and on the regional executives of Flanders and Wallonia were turned into texts for a bill on regionalization, but this bill was not submitted in parliament due to the premature end of the government.

Thus, only four of the fourteen explicit compromises were implemented peacefully. When considering the policy and conflict aspects separately, explicit compromises were more functional in terms of policy predetermination (7 cases) than in terms of conflict prevention (6 cases). Note that some of these compromises could not be implemented because the government ended prematurely. These were the two compromises that were in the process of implementation without generating new conflict.

The Freezing Effect of Procedural Implicit Compromises

Procedural arrangements were most important in the area of regionalization. One arrangement was meant to remove a point of controversy, a constitutional revision, from the agenda, which was also the actual outcome. Another procedural arrangement was more general and regarded the way in which regionalization policy would be dealt with by the coalition parties (a special parliamentary committee would be formed to consider different aspects of regionalization). Despite this arrangement being carried out immediately after the government took office, the parliamentary committee itself appeared to be unable to establish agreement on matters which were referred to it, such as delineating the boundaries of Brussels. Finally, with respect to education policy, a procedural arrangement in which certain matters were delegated to the school pact committee was carried out as agreed. In short, procedural arrangements mostly were implemented, though they actually functioned as a conflict prevention mechanism only in two of the four cases.

The Boomerang Effect of Substantive Implicit Compromises

Effects of implicit compromises of the general type were either implementation preceded by conflict, or conflict as the single outcome. The recurrence of conflict as the most visible effect is conform the expectation. Two arrangements on school policy, relating to the general fund for school construction and the fund for private schools, were elaborated successfully by the government and the National School Pact Committee, and were turned into legislation in a relatively short time. In fact, the only important compromise on education policy that was not implemented was the elaboration of a general school plan, which actually was scheduled for mid July 1973 and had to be deferred when the government broke down in January 1974. As a consequence, also the revision of the school pact had to be left to the next government.

Conflict without implementation was the most frequent effect of substantive implicit compromises, and it emerged in different fields of policy. No decisions were taken on the Brussels electoral district and on abortion, on which two bills were proposed but were left uncompleted and supported by only a part of the coalition. Finally, the conflict on state intervention in industry, which concentrated on the IBRAMCO issue, escalated into a coalition crisis.

Why did the Socialists withdraw from the government? Here, it is important to consider the relative gains and losses the coalition parties made during the process of policy making. The PSB-BSP made important concessions on different matters (education policy and language policy), and this may have meant that the costs of remaining in office were expected to exceed the benefits, especially in the view of the powerful Wallonian Labour Federation. Another reason why the party withdrew from the government may have been that the regionalists, led by party president André Cools, feared electoral punishment in the future for implementing a regionalization programme that did not have clear support of the voters in Wallonia (the coalition agreement had been approved by a narrow majority within this party). The longer the government lasted, the more the voters were expected to be driven into the arms of the more radical *Rassemblement Wallon*. This may also explain why, after the resignation of the government, the PSB-BSP was the only traditional party pressing for new parliamentary elections.

Conditions for Enforcement: Explaining Success and Failure

How can the effects of the coalition agreement be explained? What accounts for the successes and failures in enforcing the different types of compromises by the Leburton coalition? A number of favourable and unfavourable conditions for enforcement was given in chapter three. These conditions concerned the government coalition and its component parts as well as the broader environment. The underlying assumption was that parties usually do not obtain equal payoffs from individual arrangements, and that coalition agreements are not self policing. Mutual control is expected to be strongest if a coalition consists of two, unitary (undivided), parties, and participation of negotiators in the government, the existence of informal coalition governance arenas and the monitoring role of the prime minister are also seen to be favourable conditions. Finally, absence of personal rivalry and an upward economic trend also were seen to facilitate implementation of agreements.

Many compromises in the Leburton coalition agreement were not implemented because the government terminated long before the official end of its constitutional term. But most of these deferred policy decisions played a part in the increasingly troubled atmosphere within the coalition. Even matters on which no conflict had resurfaced (or at least not yet) and on which intentions were in the process of implementation were taken into account in the strategic calculations of parties. For this reason, all four types of effects analyzed in the previous section need to be taken into account when considering conditions for enforcement.

Coalition Size and Reciprocal Control

The assumption was that multi party coalitions have more problems with enforcement than two party coalitions, because with more parties the possibilities for reciprocal action are reduced. The impact of the number of parties however is not expected to be so strong that effects are either a total failure (0 percent implementation) or a total success (100 percent implementation). If failure occurs, it is seen to become more frequent over time in multi party coalitions.

Within the Leburton multi party coalition, half of the compromises were implemented, often involving conflict. Only 25 percent of the compromises was implemented without conflict. This suggests that failure was predominant, be it that this result was achieved in only one year. None the less, reciprocal control does not seem to have been very strong within the coalition – the withdrawal of the Socialists from office is an indication. The Leburton government was really successful only in the field of education policy. In other fields, arrangements were implemented less often or hardly at all.

Here, the point of payoffs for parties obtained from individual compromises is relevant. A balance may exist at the level of the coalition agreement as a whole, but parties may become impatient over time. This situation is a disincentive for continuing cooperation. In the case of the Leburton coalition, all parties expected payoffs from the coalition agreement in the first half year that the government was in office. The approval of legislation on education policy just before the summer break in 1973, however, seems to have been a critical point. After this, the CVP became increasingly reluctant to cooperate on arrangements where, especially by a group within this party, fewer payoffs were expected and major concessions had been made during government formation. The consequence was that within the PSB-BSP in particular impatience grew about the realisation of intentions in other fields. For this party, the costs of remaining in office began to exceed the benefits, up to the critical point where the decision was made to withdraw from the government. Thus, problems with enforcement seem to have been due to differences in payoffs from individual arrangements and to the structure of the agenda and the general imbalance in the distribution of policy payoffs during the first half year of the government.

Internal Party Unity

Even if coalitions contain only two parties, internal divisions within these parties also may trouble enforcement. An indicator of intraparty divisions on policy can be found in the results of party votes on the coalition agreement. Within the two largest parties, the CVP and the PSB-BSP, support was 60 percent or less. The traditional divisions within the CVP and PSC are those between the factions of labour, farmers, and the middle class, but at least with respect to the relevant parts of the coalition agreement, no major conflicts between these factions seem to have played a part. More important was a division emerging between regionalists and unitarists within the CVP and the PSB-BSP. The Socialists were not only divided along language lines, there was also a division within each language section. Within the Liberal party family, divisions in the same field existed between the Wallonian and the Brussels section (the leader of the Brussels wing of the Liberal party had voted against the coalition agreement). In this field, internal divisions thus may help explain conflict and nonimplementation, with the exception that arrangements on language policy were not contested. Enforcement of the agreement was most successful in the field where internal party rivalry was absent: education policy.

Negotiators as Ministers

What about the loyalty to the coalition agreement of ministers who participated in making the agreement? The expectation here is that those involved in policy negotiations may be able to implement more easily even in cases where commitments are left relatively vague.

The most ambitious project of the Leburton government was regionalization, and in this field ministers had not contributed directly to the coalition agreement. Conversely, the compromises on education policy were made by negotiators taking a seat in the government and they were also implemented. This was also the situation with arrangements on pensions, though the involvement of Edmund Leburton in making the deal on the oil refinery project appeared to reinforce conflict – his party's reputation was at stake.

Prime Ministerial Support

Did prime minister Leburton make a difference, either positively or negatively? Edmund Leburton was a monolingual French speaker, whose candidacy had been controversial. This reduced his influence on policy making.

Prime ministerial support for the coalition agreement varied between the different policy fields. Leburton seems to have pursued party policy actively only in the area of socio-economic policy (the IBRAMCO project), but with counter-productive results. His role seems to have been limited during implementation of the compromises on education policy, nor does it seem that success in the area of language policy can be attributed to active prime ministerial support. Leburton's rather passive role in the multiple conflicts on regionalization policy certainly did not bring peace closer. To conclude, the role of the prime minister seems more associated to coalition failure than to success.

Coalition Governance Arenas

Arenas for conflict resolution such as coalition committees are assumed to facilitate enforcement, because they are more remote from the public policy making arenas where it is immediately visible who wins and who loses.

The Leburton government was one month in office when a School Pact Committee was formed to implement the arrangements on education policy. Party presidents and responsible ministers took a seat in this committee, as well as spokespersons from other sections of the parties. The School Pact Committee seems to have contributed positively to implementation, and this condition may be seen in conjunction with the experience of ministers as negotiators and with the absence of internal party divisions in this field.

The special parliamentary committee on regionalization was another arena for policy making and conflict management. Discussions within this committee however foundered, and conflict appeared to be unmanageable. It was the government itself that had to convert the compromises on regional institutions into legislation.

Thus, only in the field of education policy did a coalition committee contribute positively to the implementation of the coalition agreement. Other informal structures within and outside the government, if these existed, did not facilitate the enforcement of arrangements – they did not contain recurring conflicts.

Economics and Personal Relationships

A factor that often is seen to encroach on the plans of decision makers is economics. The oil crisis becoming manifest in the autumn of 1973 increased the financial problems of the national government, but it also induced the Socialists to press harder for state initiatives in industry, the IBRAMCO-project being an important political test case. The withdrawal of the Iranian government from the project that induced the Socialists to withdraw from the government. In the other fields, the deteriorating state of the economy played a part more at the background. Personal clashes do not seem to have been a cause of nonenforcement of the coalition agreement.

Conclusion

The Leburton government was formed to flesh out the constitutional articles on regionalization, for which a two thirds majority in parliament was required. Though in theory this majority could be formed *ad hoc*, mistrust among the parties led them to consider regionalization sufficiently delicate to build a government coalition controlling such a large majority. Mistrust also induced the three party families to formulate explicit and implicit compromises on different aspects of regionalization. Interparty conflict was paramount during government formation. Parties differed on language policy and regionalization as well as on education policy, morality issues, and on socio-economic policy.

The 24 different compromises incorporated into the coalition agreement have not really prevented interparty conflict, and only half of them were implemented. The most difficult appeared to be the implementation of substantive implicit compromises (2 out of 6), containing intentions that are least committing. All compromises of this type worked as a boomerang; also coalition breakdown happened after conflict over intentions that were left vague. This result is conform expectations about the effects of different types of compromises. Procedures were observed in three of the four cases, and thus were functional, be it that conflict did not always remain absent. Explicit compromises had the most substantive results, but not more than in half the number of cases. Implementation of this type of compromise was peaceful in only 6 out of 14 cases, so the streamlining effect was rather limited. Generally, the relevant parts of the coalition agreement had an agenda function, and they indicated rather than predetermined coalition policy. Often, further negotiations were necessary before policies could be approved by the government and in parliament. What are called failures (i.e., no formally approved policies) may even be seen as part of a process which continued beyond the end of the government. During the formation of the next government, the central issues were those left uncompleted or undecided by the Leburton coalition.

The mixed effects of the Leburton coalition agreement may be accounted for by different factors. The absence of manifest divisions within parties and the presence of negotiators in the government are likely to have facilitated the enforcement of arrangements on the public and private school system. In the field of regionalization policy the presence of divisions and the absence of negotiators from the government were unfavourable conditions. The rather limited support of the prime minister may also have played a part. With respect to other fields, however, there have been no clear indications that prime ministerial support or opposition made a real difference to the way in which the parties dealt with compromises. Neither are there indications that strained personal relationships contributed to failure.

Coalition committees as a type of arena for coalition governance seem to have played a part, in a positive way, only in the field of education policy. Though regionalization was also dealt with in a coalition committee, discussions in this committee failed entirely, and policy making was shifted to the government (which also was unable to turn arrangements into coherent legislation). Further, a critical event from the economic environment formed the immediate cause of failure in one field, and led to the collapse of the government.

In conjunction with the above factors, reciprocal control as an enforcement mechanism seems to have been weakened, particularly by the structure of the political agenda after the summer of 1973. Within the CVP, the willingness to continue with the implementation of arrangements decreased after legislation on education policy and income policy was formally approved. As it became clear that the coalition committee on regionalization did not make much progress, the government became more important in the implementation process. The PSB-BSP, and especially the strong extraparliamentary party, became increasingly impatient about the implementation of arrangements on regionalization and issues of socio-economic policy. When the Socialists lost on the IBRAMCO-issue, early elections were considered to be necessary for preventing more policy disappointments and, as a consequence, severe electoral punishment.

Notes

1   On 23 October 1973, a reshuffle was made, in which some of the 22 ministers were replaced and 8 portfolios of state secretaries were abolished. The jurisdictions of some of the remaining ministers and state secretaries were extended.
2   Article *108 ter* of the constitution said that in the executive of the Brussels *agglomeration*, language parity was required. The present compromise, however, was for the executive of the Brussels *region*. This may illustrate the complexity of the issue.

Chapter 6

The Tindemans V Government (1977–78)

Building a Five Party Coalition

After the parliamentary elections of 17 April 1977, the leaders of the two largest parties, the Flemish CVP (Christian Democrats) and the Socialist PSB-BSP (still a unitary party), declared that they wanted a new agreement on regional and community policy. Ambitions extended to a revision of the constitution, which should be realized during the next legislative term.[1] According to the CVP, the Socialists were needed to build a broad governmental majority for economic austerity policy and, even more important, for meeting the constitutional requirement of a qualified and special majority in approving legislation on regionalization based on constitutional article *107 quater*.[2] As we saw, the Leburton coalition had made no progress on institutional reform and regionalization, and the governments in office between 1974 and 1977 also foundered on the issue.

CVP-prominent Leo Tindemans was instructed to form a new government. The first move in coalition building was made by PSB-president André Cools, who successfully prevented that the Liberals participated in the negotiations. The CVP, PSC and PSB-BSP however had only just a two thirds majority, and this made the party leaders consider participation of a regionalist party. But the constitutional requirement of language parity in the cabinet made it necessary to take two regionalist parties on board, one from the Dutch speaking part and a French speaking party.

The Flemish People's Union (VU) and the Democratic Front of French speakers (FDF) were invited, but a condition made by *formateur* Tindemans was that they should accept an agreement on regionalization made by the other parties. This procedure reflected the rather lukewarm support from Tindemans of a coalition including regionalists, and the VU and FDF rejected this condition. The alternative followed was that that the five parties first discussed the general points and then negotiate the controversial issues.

The formation process lasted six weeks, of which only two and a half were actually spent on the coalition agreement, with the focus on regionalization policy. With 12,600 words, the coalition agreement was shorter than that of the Leburton government. The document consisted of two separate parts, the first dealing with regionalization, and referred to as the *Egmont Pact*, after the name of the palace where it was negotiated. The second part of the agreement contained mainly arrangements on socio-economic policy.

The Egmont pact was a relatively detailed document, more detailed that the section on regionalization policy in the Leburton agreement – the parties felt that negotiated agreement could reduce the costs of decision making later on. The first paragraph of the pact stated that the coalition parties were morally committed to the intentions on constitutional reform and accomplishing regionalization. As the government could not carry out such a constitutional reform, the pact was meant to commit not only the present government but also the next one. Prime minister Tindemans however was sceptical, and stated that the agreement could mean 'both war and peace' (Luykx & Platel, 1985: 697).

The coalition agreement was approved at the party conferences in May 1977. Support varied, though not as much as in the Leburton coalition. The regionalist parties were least supportive, with a two thirds majority voting yes. Within the CVP, the new prime minister Leo Tindemans and party president Wilfried Martens were leading different groups with tensed relationships in the field of regionalization. On 3 June 1977, the Tindemans V government took office.

Turning Policy Conflicts into Deals

The coalition agreement contained a part on socio-economic policy and the Egmont Pact on regionalization. This reflected the coalition formation agenda, dominated by conflicts in these two fields.

Regionalization Policy

Regionalization policy was the first major problem inherited from the previous government. More specifically, direct confrontations between the prospective coalition parties were on the composition and competencies of regional bodies, financial resources of the regions and on decision making bodies of the language communities. Other subjects of manifest controversy were implementation procedures, the role of the provinces, and the boundaries of Brussels. As in the agreement of the Leburton government, a distinction was made between arrangements meant to be transitional and more definitive arrangements. Generally, the positions of the traditional parties had not changed much since the Leburton government, which as we saw had not achieved much in this area.

Regional bodies   With regard to the composition of the regional bodies, the parties agreed that after a transitional period, the regional councils of Flanders and Wallonia would consist of directly elected representatives. The size of these regional councils was to be the same as the number of *parliamentary* representatives elected in the same region. The Brussels regional council however was to consist of twice the number of parliamentary representatives from Brussels. Within the Brussels regional council, the so called *alarm bell procedure* could be started. This benefited the Flemish parties, as these formed a minority in Brussels. Further, French speaking and Dutch speaking cultural committees should be created in Brussels, which were to be elected by the two language groups within the Brussels regional council. This was an explicit compromise also mentioning further details on the election procedure.

Another explicit compromise was formulated on the executive bodies of Wallonia and Flanders, the regional governments, of which the members were to be elected by and from within the regional councils. The Brussels executive body was to consist of a maximum of seven members, including at least two Dutch speakers. This meant that the principle of language parity (an equal number of French speakers and Dutch speakers) would not be upheld. This constituted an important payoff for the French speaking parties, in particular the FDF.

Regional finance and competencies With respect to regional competencies, a detailed explicit compromise was hammered out. The Brussels regional council would take over the existing competencies of the agglomeration council, which would be abolished (Luykx & Platel, 1985: 700). With regard to the financial resources of the regions, party preferences differed most on the distributive aspect and on the possibility of introducing regional taxes. Another explicit compromise was made which stated that regional taxation would be introduced, be it only in the definitive stage of regionalization, so not during the term of this government. Further, subsidies from the central government to the regions were to be distributed as follows: one third in proportion to population, one third in proportion to area, and one third in proportion to direct taxes. Here, not only party positions had remained largely the same, but also the results of bargaining, as four years earlier essentially the same arrangement was made. These subsidies would be linked to the annual increase in the national budget.

Community bodies A next issue was the composition and competencies of the bodies representing the language communities. If regionalization was a problem of territory and economic decentralization, the communities were relevant for language and cultural matters. With respect to the composition of the community bodies, the parties reached an explicit compromise which stated that the community councils (thus far called cultural councils) would consist of regional representatives, including also the members of the two language groups in the Brussels regional council. This implied that there would be an overlap in membership of the community councils and the regional councils. Yet, the two bodies would have different competencies. This was a major concession from the VU and a group within the CVP that had preferred a complete merger of the regional councils and community councils in Flanders.

An explicit compromise was also reached on the executive body of the communities. This body was to contain two members, elected 'by and from within' the community councils, but they were supposed to come from different regional councils, and one from the Brussels regional council. With regard to the language communities in the Brussels region, a special procedure was created. Each of the 19 municipalities in Brussels was to set up two community committees, of which the members were to be elected in municipal elections (the exact size of the committees was left open). The committees were to advise their respective municipalities on matters belonging to the competence of the communities (cultural matters), and they also were to control the expenses of the communities within the municipalities.

Community finance and competencies With regard to the competencies of the community bodies, a particularly thorny issue was the definition of the 'matières personalisables' – matters next to the cultural affairs on which the communities already had competence. This extension was to increase what was called the cultural autonomy of the communities. Such autonomy was strongly desired on the Flemish side, but the French speaking parties, especially the PSB, wanted to maintain a number of transferable tasks, such as health, at the level of the central government. The reason for this was mainly financial. The PSB conceded on this issue, the result being an explicit compromise stating that competencies, also on health, would be attributed to the communities.

Financial resources were, as before, to be provided by the central government, the contested point this time being the new distribution ratio. The main difference between the parties concerned the relative weight of population size as a criterion. The Dutch speaking parties would benefit from more emphasis on this factor, whereas the French speaking parties demanded that more weight be given to area size. On this point again an explicit compromise was reached which stated that in the new distribution of subsidies resources would depend for two thirds on population size, and for one third on area size.

Implementation procedures and transitional arrangements   Most of the arrangements mentioned in the paragraphs above were meant to be implemented after a revision of the constitution during the *next* parliamentary term (which normally would begin in 1981). Negotiations were also undertaken on the status of the regional and community bodies during a transition period. The parties made an explicit compromise. Three bills would be drafted, which were to be submitted in parliament 'as soon as possible'. The first bill was about the implementation of article *107 quater* of the constitution. The second bill was on the extension of cultural matters to the 'matières personalisables' mentioned before. The third bill was to modify existing legislation on language in administrative affairs.

The first bill in particular was of great political importance. It was to contain a chapter on definitive arrangements, to which the condition of a constitutional revision was linked, and a chapter on transitional arrangements, which would remain valid until the new regional councils and executives were set up – but no longer than until one year after the next parliamentary elections. In this transition stage, the regional councils of Wallonia and Flanders were to consist of members of the national parliament. The Brussels regional council was to be composed of representatives and senators from both language groups in parliament. Further, regional financial resources would consist entirely of subsidies from the national government.

Provinces and subregions   A next point on the formation agenda was the future status of the provinces and the creation of subregions. Disagreement existed on whether these subregions were to exist next to the other administrative entities, or were to replace the provinces. In an explicit compromise the parties agreed that subregions would be set up after the transition stage of regionalization, and that the role of the provinces would be reduced. The main conceding parties on this issue were the PSC and FDF.

Boundaries of the Brussels region   Delimitation of the Brussels region was kept for the final round of negotiations, to avoid that stalemate on this matter would hinder agreement on other issues of regionalization. The French speaking parties advocated unconstrained expansion of Brussels, and at the very least an extension of the facilities for French speakers in the municipalities in the Brussels periphery. Dutch speakers spoke of a Brussels oil slick which had to be contained, and for this reason they wanted to limit the new region to the 19 officially bilingual municipalities. More specifically, the FDF and PSC demanded the annexation of six municipalities with facilities for French speakers (these were located in the Flemish province of Brabant, an important geographical and political fact) as well as of four separate districts on the periphery of the agglomeration.

On this final issue, the parties also managed to compromise explicitly. This compromise was based partly on an agreement made several years earlier, but which never was implemented. It included the possibility for French speakers in the six peripheral municipalities and in several other areas to take fictitious domicile in one of the 19 official municipalities of Brussels. In this way they obtained the right to vote in the elections for that municipality, and also partly obtained the same rights and duties on administrative, judicial and fiscal matters as the 'official' Brussels residents. The government was to decide how long this right would exist. A second element of the compromise contained the extension of facilities for the French speakers in the six municipalities to the cultural and personal matters defined earlier in the arrangement on community councils. These points however were gained at a price: on the boundaries of Brussels, the status quo would be maintained (the Brussels region thus would be the agglomeration of 19 municipalities). A third element was the division of the Brussels electoral district. This division had been blocked by the French speaking parties, for example during the formation of the Leburton government in early 1973.

Socio-economic Policy

Though the parties wanted to deal less with the details of socio-economic policy, there were some issues on which manifest conflict existed. These issues were the budget deficit, the coupling of wages and social benefits to economic development, employment policy, and state intervention in industry, which divided mainly the two traditional party families, Christian Democrats and Socialists. On this last matter, they had rather unpleasant experiences during the Leburton government.

To begin with, the Socialists demanded extra taxes to decrease the budget deficit. This demand was rejected most firmly by *formateur* Tindemans himself, who even threatened to withdraw if tax increases would be placed on the government agenda (De Standaard, 17–25 May 1977). Negotiations on this matter resulted in a substantive implicit compromise.

Another claim made by the Socialists was that wages and social benefits be linked directly to the consumer price index. The other parties gave way on this point, which was written down in the coalition agreement. Less clear cut were intentions on employment policy. Here, the PSB-BSP demanded an employment plan, which was received with considerable scepticism by the CVP. A substantive implicit compromise was formulated, and the government would have the task of fleshing this out.

Finally, as in the Leburton coalition, Socialists and Christian Democrats disagreed on state intervention in industry and in the banking sector. The Flemish Christian Democrats, including *formateur* Tindemans, were suspicious of Socialist attempts to increase state control in these areas. On this point of contention the parties got no further than formulating a rather opaque substantive implicit compromise, stating that the government would be active in different sectors of the economy 'on the basis of equality with the private sector'. Table 6.1 contains the compromises made on issues in the two policy fields. Note that, for the set of controversial issues considered here, no procedural implicit compromises were made.

Table 6.1   Arrangements in Tindemans V coalition agreement

	Type of arrangement		Total
	explicit	substantive implicit	
Policy field			
regionalization	11	–	11
budget	–	1	1
socio-economic	1	2	3
	12	3	15

Putting Deals into Practice

Compared to the Leburton coalition agreement, the Tindemans V agreement contained fewer deals, but a very large proportion (12 out of 15) of these deals were explicit compromises. No substantive implicit compromises were made on controversial points, so the Egmont Pact on regionalization was, in principle, a doable programme. But was this also the case in practice? And how have the parties proceeded in implementing the relatively vague intentions on socio-economic policy?

Regionalization Policy

One month after the government took office, an amendment of the 'Act on a provisional setup of the regional bodies' (1974) was approved in parliament. The amendment was necessary to make the Act compatible with the coalition agreement. In the coalition agreement a bill for the transitional stage of regionalization was announced, giving an outline of the proposed bill. Parliament also approved a bill in which the elections of the Brussels agglomeration council were suspended. This bill was based on the intention in the coalition agreement to abolish the agglomeration council, the functions of which were to be taken over by the Brussels regional council (KHA, 1977: 457).

The coalition agreement contained three bills which were to encompass the elements of the Egmont pact. One bill was to comprise the extended list of cultural matters, concerning the communities, and one covered the use of language in the administration. The third bill regarded the implementation of article *107 quater* of the constitution containing the creation of three regions.

In the late summer of 1977, the government set out to translate arrangements from the Egmont pact into bills. Soon, a difference of interpretation occurred on the meaning of the arrangement for the subscription right for French speakers in the Brussels periphery. According to one of the state secretaries of Institutional Reform, De Bondt (CVP), the subscription right was meant to be used only once in the near future. This interpretation was contested by the PSC and FDF. In their view, the agreement contained no indication of a time limit, and that the subscription right was permanent. Thus, conflict emerged over an explicit compromise.

More conflicts occurred. One was on the future status of the subregions, on which an explicit compromise had been formulated. Another conflict regarded the community committees in the Brussels municipalities and their functional equivalents in the periphery. More specifically, controversy existed on the size of these committees and on the distribution of subsidies between the two language groups in the municipalities. Third, the arrangement on the composition of the regional executives was seen to need further elaboration. Here, one problem was that the French and Dutch version of the same arrangement appeared to give rise to different interpretations (KHA, 1978: 53–54). Thus, turning the Egmont pact into draft bills first required exegesis of the document.

From one pact to the other, but no legislation In September 1977, a special committee was set up, containing the party presidents, some other spokespersons from the parties, the two state secretaries of Institutional Reform, and the prime minister, who would be the chair. This informal group was called the 'editorial committee', and was to interpret the arrangements and 'fill in the possible gaps' in the Egmont pact (KHA, 1977: 707). Policy making was thus transferred from the formal decision making bodies to an informal arena. The expected result of the work by the committee was that the bill on regionalization could be submitted in parliament without further delay (Brassine & Mabille, 1978: 9–11; KHA, 1977: 742–743).

Though most party presidents continued to declare that the Egmont agreement was to be implemented without making trouble, and Tindemans emphasized that the parties had committed themselves to refrain from making other proposals not just in one but in *two* parliamentary terms, the discussions soon took on the character of new negotiations, and lasted four months. The result was a new document named the Stuyvenberg pact (Platel, 1978: 448, 454). At the end of February 1978, the document was ratified by the cabinet, with parliamentary approval following one month later (KHA, 1978: 199).

The Stuyvenberg pact contained extended and often more specific arrangements on matters which had given rise to conflict. Next, the government again faced the task of translating intentions into texts for the draft bill, named Bill 461. This was done first for the arrangements for the transitional period, for which no revision of the constitution was required. Discussions were painstaking, particularly over the community committees in the six municipalities around Brussels, the subscription right, and the decision making procedures in the Brussels regional executive. Only after frequent interventions by what was called the 'junta of party presidents', could Bill 461 be completed. In early July, it was approved by the cabinet and subsequently submitted in parliament. In the Chamber of Representatives, the bill was examined by a parliamentary committee chaired by Wilfried Martens (who also was party president of the CVP). In fact, nearly the whole junta of party presidents had a seat in the parliamentary committee (Brassine & Mabille: 13).

The parliamentary committee, however, was unable to proceed in line with the timeschedule. First, at the end of July, the Council of State (a constitutional advisory body of the government) gave a negative advice on several articles in Bill 461. The Council of State even declared some articles unconstitutional, notably those based on the rather complex compromises over Brussels. The reactions of the party leaders were rather different. Prime minister Tindemans preferred to follow at least the main lines of the advice, but PSB president Cools suggested to ignore it. In his view, the political will of the party presidents was not less important than the constitution. This pressure had effect, as the cabinet decided not to engage in a reformulation of the relevant articles, at least not on a short term. This however did not lead to consensus within the parliamentary committee, which was unable to vote on a first part of Bill 461 (KHA, 1978: 553).

Also an article containing the possibility of a *de facto* merger of the regional councils and community councils was heavily disputed. The problem was that such a merger (considered only in the Flemish case) went beyond what was written in the Egmont-Stuyvenberg pact, but was mentioned explicitly in the bill. The French speaking parties insisted that this article was amended. Again, the party presidents met and made a compromise on which the possibility of joint meetings of the Flemish regional and community councils was included, as long as these meetings would not be in Brussels (De Standaard, 5–11 September 1978). At the end of September 1977, the parliamentary committee approved the amended bill, so that plenary discussions could be started.

This prefixed agreement within the committee, however, did not prevent that a group within the parliamentary party of the CVP, and with the support of the prime minister, made objections to several articles in the bill. The group decided not to vote for Bill 461 as long as it contained elements called unconstitutional by the Council of State. This was a problem, as the government was not competent to revise the constitution during its term in office. When Tindemans did not establish discipline within his party, the French speaking ministers threatened to withdraw from the government. On 11 October 1978, the party presidents of the PSB, PSC and VU attacked the prime minister, who subsequently resigned and thus brought down the government.

Budgetary and Socio-economic Policy

In contrast to the Egmont pact, arrangements in the fields of financial and socio-economic policy mostly were substantive implicit compromises.

During the first half year in office, socio-economic policy was elaborated and implemented in accordance with the coalition agreement, and without real political difficulties. The Socialists, who had made most demands but had to accept rather general arrangements, declared to be satisfied with the way these intentions were elaborated (KHA, 1977: 678).

Problems however began to rise in early 1978, when the government was confronted with a massive gap between the prognosis and the actual budget deficit:

65 billion Bf. instead of 24 billion (KHA, 1978: 136). Decisions to give financial support to several industries in Flanders and Wallonia were made in line with the coalition agreement, but the parties had difficulty agreeing on retrenchment policy. The government had announced a bill on economic and budgetary policy, which was to be submitted in parliament before the end of May 1978. To the prime minister, this was important enough to declare that the government could only remain in office if parliament approved the bill without delay, but first of all, consensus was to be reached within the government. The ministers of the CVP stressed that cutbacks in expenditures should have priority, and that taxes should decrease. The state secretary of the Budget (also CVP) asked for far reaching special discretionary powers for the government, thus circumventing parliamentary approval. The PSB-BSP as well as the VU however opposed such special powers, and declared that economic reforms and the extension of state control in different sectors of the economy should have more emphasis. Moreover, the FDF and the French speaking Socialists insisted that the bill on economic and budgetary policy be submitted in parliament together with Bill 461 on regionalization. In the view of the prime minister, this issue linkage was 'pure blackmail'.

These disputes almost led to a government crisis. According to prime minister Tindemans, the Socialists were not cooperative, and on 14 June 1978 he tendered the resignation of the government. The King however refused, and instructed Tindemans settle the dispute. Also the party presidents preferred a continuation of the government to speed up regionalization policy making. The conflict was resolved in a joint meeting of the cabinet committee on economic and social policy and the party presidents, in which it was decided that the bill on economic policy would be submitted and approved in parliament before the summer break. The bill on economic policy was submitted, and was approved in late June 1977. The two key elements in the bill were public investments and state control in different sectors of the economy, and the delegation of special powers to the government. The first element entailed gains for the Socialists, and the second for the CVP (KHA, 1978: 425–426; Luykx & Platel: 712–713).

Effects of the Coalition Agreement

Table 6.2 summarizes the effects of the Tindemans V coalition agreement in terms of conflict prevention and policy prefiguration. Clearly, the coalition agreement hardly was functional in these ways. Conflict on previously contested issues resurfaced more often than not, and of the intentions laid down in the different parts of the agreement, only few were implemented. As in the case of the Leburton government, the premature end of the government also made it virtually impossible to implement the whole coalition agreement, but, as in that case, this was not just an unlucky coincidence. It was the result of strategic choices made by coalition parties.

This overall effect may be considered more closely in regard of the expectations on the types of compromises. These more detailed findings are summarized in table 6.3, and are analyzed below.

Table 6.2   Effects of Tindemans V coalition agreement

		Implementation		Total
		+	−	
conflict prevention	+	1	5	6
	−	3	6	9
		4	11	15

Table 6.3   Effects of types of arrangements

	Type of arrangement			Total
	explicit	procedural	substantive	
Effect				
implemented no conflict	1 (so-ed)	−	−	1
not implemented no conflict	5 (reg)	−	−	5
implemented conflict	−	−	3 (bud, so-ec)	3
not implemented conflict	6 (reg)	−	−	6
	12	−	3	15

The Streamlining Effect of Explicit Compromises

Explicit compromises were almost never implemented (only 1 out of 12 was implemented, the linkage between wages and the consumer price index), though conflict as a form of failure was less frequent; 6 compromises on regionalization involved conflict, and 5, also all on regionalization policy, did not involve new conflict. On these points, the explicit compromises did streamline policy making within the government before parliamentary discussions started.

None the less, in this field of policy, paralysis is the most important result. A number of intentions were in the process of implementation, but the premature end of the government was related also to these points. They comprised a policy project that influential forces within the coalition did not want to bring to a successful end. The conclusion thus is that developments in the Tindemans V government provide no evidence for the assumed streamlining effect of explicit compromises.

Covell (1982: 457) has argued that it was the symmetry of the agenda after the resolution of problems on socio-economic policy (summer 1978) which made a coalition crisis inevitable. A direct confrontation on the Brussels issue existed, in which the claims of one party were the most resisted concessions of the other. Dissent within the CVP formed an extra complication. For the dissenters within this party (with the implicit support of prime minister Tindemans), coalition breakdown was not the worst possible outcome. Elections would delay regionalization, and elections also were expected to benefit the CVP, which could then attack the VU for having sold out Flemish regional interests.

The Boomerang Effect of Substantive Implicit Compromises

During the first half year of the government, financial and budgetary policy decisions were made without real political difficulties, but things changed during the second half year. At stake was legislation on budgetary policy and on the regulation of state intervention in different sectors of the economy, matters on which the parties had agreed only implicitly. A government crisis could be resolved only with the help of the party presidents. Under the external guidance of these party presidents, the government reached agreement on legislation, which was eventually approved in parliament. Thus, in the field of financial and socio-economic policy, the parties elaborated the coalition agreement and were able to turn intentions into decisions. This involved conflict, as was expected for this type of compromise, but the successful implementation stands out compared to the dramatic effects of explicit compromises. Thus, the substantive implicit compromises worked as a boomerang, but they did not lead to a knock out of policy makers.

Conditions for Enforcement: Explaining Success and Failure

The problem of enforcement was particularly salient during the Tindemans V government. Hardly any success in implementing the coalition agreement was reached, except in the field of socio-economic policy where the deals were put into practice shortly after the government took office. For the other matters, a longer time horizon was necessary, but not possible for political reasons. Political conflict became manifest in different ways, and the conditions for enforcement relate to this.

Coalition Size and Reciprocal Control

The first condition assumed to be unfavourable was the multi party character of the coalition. Coalitions containing three or more parties were expected to have a lower capacity for reciprocal control. Limited payoffs from particular arrangements in combination were expected to increase the temptation for parties to ignore partly or completely commitments made during government formation. With five parties, centralization and discipline in implementation is more difficult to achieve.

In the field of financial and socio-economic policy, conflict was mainly between the two traditional party families, particularly the CVP and the PSB. The CVP, represented in this case by the party's prime minister, threatened the PSB-BSP with a crisis if no substantive policies were approved before the end of the parliamentary year in 1978. Conversely, the PSB demanded observation of the explicit compromises on regionalization, which however required more time to be turned into legislation. The presence of two regionalist parties – the fourth and fifth party in the coalition – made a difference in that they pressed for more far reaching institutional changes than originally agreed. This contrasted with the anti federal position taken by part of the CVP, for which even the coalition agreement already contained too many painful concessions. The five parties thus were extremely difficult to turn into a tight coalition, and centrifugal forces undermined the possibilities of enforcement.

Internal Party Unity

For one thing, the CVP was strongly divided internally over regionalization policy. Unitarists led by prime minister Tindemans and federalists guided by party president Wilfried Martens, prominent during government formation, were beginning to clash. The officially still unitary PSB-BSP was also divided on regionalization – the party split into a separate Dutch speaking and a French speaking party shortly after the government ended. Failure in this field thus can be attributed in part to internal party disunity. This contrasts to the situation in the field of socio-economic policy, where (despite the presence of institutionalized factions within the traditional parties) no intraparty divisions became manifest during policy making.

Negotiators as Ministers

Did the presence or absence of negotiators in the Tindemans V government make a difference? Most ministers for whom regionalization was within their jurisdiction had not been involved in the negotiations on the coalition agreement. One state secretary of Institutional Reform even was a spokesman of a local branch of the CVP that had voted against the Egmont pact (De Ridder, 1982: 270). Only in the area of financial and socio-economic policy had ministers experienced policy negotiations.

The relationship between this structural government property and the effects of the coalition agreement is consistent to what was expected. Failure occurred where ministers were confronted with prefixed compromises as *faits accomplis*, and success was reached in the field where deals were made by party spokespeople who took a seat in the government. Though failure did not always occur in the government but also in the parliamentary and extraparliamentary arenas, this pattern in the Tindemans V government suggests that ministerial background made a difference for enforcement.

Prime Ministerial Support

The prime minister played different roles in the enforcement process. He guided the elaboration of the coalition agreement in the field of socio-economic policy, with success. If perhaps not an activist in the sense of making substantive proposals, he certainly facilitated the elaboration of the coalition agreement, and even threatened with a crisis to speed things up.

This contrasts rather sharply with the role of Leo Tindemans in the field of regionalization policy. As a *formateur*, Tindemans already spoke of the Egmont pact as a pact of party presidents, which he signed with reluctance (De Ridder, 1982: 133). Later, he often called in the help of the party presidents, and even proposed to delegate the drafting of legislation to them. Though he did not approve the prominence of the party presidents in policy making, this behaviour resulted directly from his unwillingness to bear responsibility for the regionalization programme, which he called unconstitutional and in his view went against the interests of the CVP in the national political institutions. The decision to tender the resignation of the government also may be seen in this light. In short, in addition to the previous factor of ministerial background, prime ministerial support, and absence of support, is likely to have been a relevant condition for enforcement.

Coalition Governance Arenas

One of the remarkable things about the Tindemans V coalition was the presence of what was called the 'junta' of party presidents as an informal arena of coalition governance (Dewinter, Timmermans and Dumont, 2000: 328). This group became active during government formation. According to one author, the party presidents, who had negotiated the Egmont pact in absolute secrecy, had become alienated from the rest of their party, even from those within the party who were *ministrable* (De Ridder, 1982: 138; 1989: 109–122).

The paradoxical situation in the Tindemans government was that successes occurred in the fields in which arenas for managing high politics and conflicts do not seem to have played a part, whereas the transfer of policy making to such informal arenas did not prevent that conflict and policy failure was the effect. It was after discussions were shifted to the parliamentary arena that conflicts began to escalate. There, the party presidents also lost control of the process. In short, the dramatic developments during the term in office of the Tindemans V government show that presence of coalition committees as arenas of conflict management is not a sufficient condition for success.

Economics and Personal Relationships

Personal relationships were seen to play a part if manifest personal clashes occurred between party prominents. Such tensions have existed. In fact, the manoeuvres made by prime minister Tindemans during the last days of the government cannot be understood fully without considering personal relationships. There was strong antagonism between the prime minister and PSB president André Cools, and also between the prime minister and the president of his own party serious tensions frustrated policy making on important issues, and speedup of coalition breakdown (De Ridder, 1982: 206).

Finally, the economic situation did not allow budget expansion, and this constrained the possibilities of implementing arrangements involving major expenses. Most of these arrangements, however, were left relatively general (the ones on socio-economic policy almost all were implicit compromises). Thus the CVP demanded cutbacks, whereas the Socialists pressed for financial injections for troubled industries (in the French speaking region in particular) and for an active employment policy. Conflict escalated into a coalition crisis in June 1978, which however was resolved and subsequently a package of austerity policy including special powers for the government was adopted. The broader agenda of regionalization involved issues of redistribution, but the most intense conflicts in this field were on constitutional and jurisdictional aspects of Bill 461. None the less, the economic situation was part of the problem definition by the coalition parties, and as such it severely reduced the leeway for implementation of policy ambitions.

Conclusion

For a coalition involving five parties, the scope of policy bargaining during the formation of the Tindemans V government was relatively limited. The main reason for this seems to be that policy in the area of regionalization formed the *raison d'être* of the government. Moreover, two of the five parties – the regionalist VU and FDF – profiled themselves mainly in this area.

The two main fields of policy dealt with during government formation, socio-economic policy and *la question communautaire*, also dominated the agenda of the Tindemans V government after taking office. In this sense, the coalition agreement very clearly constituted an agenda for the government – but one of great political misfortune. The many explicit compromises did not prevent conflict, and the process of implementation of the plans on regionalization got stuck during parliamentary discussions. Of the 15 compromises made during government formation, only 6 did not generate new conflict. Less than one third of the compromises was implemented. Contrary to the expected effects, just 1 out of the 12 explicit compromises was implemented, but all 3 substantive implicit compromises were implemented. The coalition agreement thus hardly was functional in terms of policy streamlining. It functioned as an agenda, but the parties were opportunistic in dealing with the intentions as agreed during government formation. Though restatements of policy intentions also may be seen as a pragmatic approach, the trouble in the Tindemans V government was that the parties disagreed completely, and even disagreed internally, about the direction such policy restatements should go.

A factor that played a part in the stagnated process of enforcement was the general economic situation, which induced parties to fight hard for what they thought were the appropriate ways of interpreting general goals in the field of socio-economic policy. None the less, in this field, absence of internal party divisions and ministerial experience as participants in government formation seem to have contributed to the achievements of the government. In addition, prime ministerial pressure, if somewhat overstrained (threat to resign), also helped the government to accomplish policy decisions. Since rather different views of financial and socio-economic policy existed within the coalition, the centrifugal effects of the size of the coalition, with five parties, seems to have been limited by these factors.

It seems to be more than a coincidence that failures occurred in the field where negotiators were absent from the government, the traditional parties were internally divided and the position of the prime minister varied between halfhearted support and open opposition to the coalition agreement. To this, we may add that personal relationships between party prominents were becoming more and more strained. Gains and losses made in the field of regionalization weighed heavily on all coalition parties, and no party was in a position to enforce cooperation, nor was prime minister Tindemans willing to do this.

Though the party presidents were very prominent here, their mostly informal actions were not sufficient to guide legislation on regionalization through parliament. Covell (1982) has argued that differences between informal and formal policy making arenas were important. After informal discussions on the Egmont Pact during government formation, and later during the Stuyvenberg negotiations were completed, implementation stagnated within the formal decision making arenas of the government and parliament. In the parliamentary arena, the public visibility of gains and losses in policy making reinforced intransigence, particularly within the CVP. For this reason, the end of the Tindemans V government is a clear example of the general point that strategic party goals often are more important than coalition maintenance.

Notes

1 For a constitutional revision, parliament must be *constituent*, which requires a special declaration by the outgoing government before the elections. The recently elected parliament was not constituent.
2 That is, a two thirds majority in parliament and at the same time a simple majority in each of the two language groups.

Chapter 7

The Van Agt II Government (1981–82)

Building a Three Party Coalition

In the parliamentary elections of 27 May 1981, the three largest parties all lost votes. The outgoing government parties CDA (Christian Democrats) and VVD (Liberals) lost their majority. The main opposition party, the PvdA (Social Democrats) however also lost votes. The electoral winner was D66 (Liberal Democrats), and this result meant that it was likely to play a role in the next government formation. This party however publicly rejected cooperation with the incumbent two parties, and thus the main question was whether the PvdA and D66 should be included in a new coalition. The PvdA however did not want to govern together with the VVD. Earlier experiences in a coalition containing both PvdA and CDA (1973–1977, and in 1977, in a protracted and failed government formation attempt) were traumatic, and had led to deep mutual mistrust. In 1981, distances between the policy preferences of the PvdA and CDA on financial and socio-economic policy were larger than the gap between the CDA and VVD. Coalition building thus became a typical Dutch puzzle.

The combination CDA-PvdA-D66 was preferred most by the CDA, the largest party, and the PvdA. D66 not only had won in the elections, but for the CDA its inclusion also reduced the relative weight of the PvdA. The PvdA considered D66 a reliable partner in a coalition with the CDA. Between these three parties, policy negotiations were initiated. The approach was that general discussions on several fields of policy would be held first, followed by negotiations on controversial matters. The second round had a tense opening, as the PvdA presented 6 major policy claims taken from the election manifesto. These claims were: (1) a decrease in income differences, (2) no decrease in spending power of the lowest income groups, (3) equal opportunities for men and women, including individualizaton of incomes, (4) elaboration of a plan for the creation of 300,000 jobs, (5) the closing down of the two nuclear power stations in the Netherlands, and finally (6) the reduction of military nuclear tasks from six to four and denouncement of the deployment of cruise missiles in the Netherlands. For the PvdA, agreement on these issues was a *conditio sine qua non* for government participation. This last point was felt more generally, because for the other parties the 6 issues also were salient. Since they took different positions, agreement indeed was a necessary condition for the three coalition to be viable. Another salient and controversial issue was reform of the secondary education system.

Government formation was a relay race of informateurs and formateurs who had difficulty bringing the process to a successful end. The parties negotiated a basic agreement but consensus on this document was more apparent than real. The most contested point was a fundamental one: the alleged incompatibility of major cuts in spending on the one hand (demanded by the CDA) and ambitious plans with financial injections for reducing unemployment on the other (the claims of the PvdA). Within the CDA, however, a difference emerged between Dries van Agt as the party leader and first spokesman in the negotiations and the other members of the parliamentary group on the need of cuts in expenses. This tension prolonged the negotiations on the coalition agreement, which were concluded at the end of August 1981.

The coalition agreement was a document of 15,900 words, entailing what were called the 'results of the programme discussions' and a number of supplementary 'programme conclusions'. The scope of the agreement was broad, but not many intentions were really specific and doable. As one of the *informateurs* noted: 'Sometimes, few words were needed for important questions and many words for less important matters' (HTK, 1981, 17000/2: 5). The key issue of course was whether with this coalition agreement and once in office, the parties would need many words for the important matters. The Van Agt II government took office on 11 September 1981.

Turning Policy Conflicts into Deals

Budgetary and Socio-economic Policy

During the formation, financial and socio-economic policy was important both because of the deteriorating economic situation and because the three parties had profiled themselves rather differently in this field. During the negotiations, the focus was on cuts in expenditures, the budget deficit, elaboration of an employment plan, income and tax policy, and investment regulation.

The budget deficit and cuts in expenses   Though the three parties did not show large differences in their preferences with regard to the budget deficit in the long run, dissent existed over the goals for 1982 and 1983. For PvdA leader Joop den Uyl, the limit of tolerance on this matter was an attempt to reduce the deficit in 1982 and 1983, but he did not want to commit his party to concrete results. CDA leader Dries van Agt, on the other hand, insisted that all parties commit themselves to a decrease of the budget deficit by 1 percent in 1982, and 1 percent in 1983. D66 concurred with this view. An explicit compromise on this matter was formulated, containing an intention to decrease the deficit by 1 percent in 1982 and 1 percent in 1983. This entailed a payoff for the CDA. This compromise however mentioned nothing about the following years (1984 and 1985).

The next, and closely related, point was the size of cuts in government expenditures. CDA leader Van Agt demanded cuts amounting to Dfl. 4.5 billion in 1982. Both the PvdA and D66 rejected this claim. According to D66, fixing exact amounts was something to be left to the new government, not to be written down in a coalition agreement. The PvdA linked the matter to the employment plan, on which the discussions had not led to concrete results. Here, the CDA made concessions. Neither the claim of 4.5 billion (referred to as Van Agt's dowry, because he was the outgoing prime minister) nor any other specific amount of cuts for 1982 was mentioned in the coalition agreement. Agreement was reached only on the size of cuts for the whole four year term of the government period: 9.5 billion, which would be enforced 'with the emphasis on the first two years of the government'. This entailed a substantive implicit compromise.

A distribution ratio for cutbacks in the major sectors of government spending also was included. These sectors were social security (mainly the responsibility of the ministry of Social Affairs & Employment), health (ministry of Health), public sector wages (Internal Affairs) and other departmental spending. This cutback ratio was 3:1:3:2 for the four sectors, and it regarded the whole four year period. It was agreed also that new policy could be developed only if it did not involve claims for extra money. New expenses were to be compensated by cuts on other matters. In the view of Van Agt, these points in the coalition agreement formed 'an extra lock on the door' to prevent the PvdA from steering towards increases in spending 'for particular purposes' (he meant the employment plan).

A final point was abut the tax burden, which according to the CDA should be stabilized at the level of 1980. The PvdA however preferred to make an exception for expected revenues from anti fraud policy, higher costs of public services, increases in gas prices and, especially, spending on employment. The CDA advocated a broader definition, and firmly rejected the exception of spending on employment, which in the view of the Christian Democrats would make the whole intention a farce. Negotiations on this point resulted in a explicit compromise stipulating that the tax burden would be fixed at the level of 1981 (62.1 percent of the national income; but corrected for revenues from gas sales it was 55.1 percent). The first points mentioned by the PvdA (anti fraud revenues, costs of public services) were also incorporated into the coalition agreement, but not the last two (gas price increases and spending on employment). This meant that an important financial constraint on employment policy was built in into the coalition agreement.

The employment plan   Rapidly growing unemployment induced all three parties to make this problem one of the new government's key points of attention. But bargaining on financial and budgetary policy did not lead to consensus over the approach for reducing unemployment. As said, one of the key issues, and according to the PvdA a raison d'être of the new government, was an employment plan, a typical piece of Keynesian policy. CDA and D66 agreed to mention in the agreement that such a plan would be developed, but the CDA refused to make any further commitments. The arrangement thus was an implicit compromise, which mentioned that an employment plan would be elaborated within 4 months after the government had taken office.

Income and tax policy   The CDA and the PvdA disagreed also on developments for the lowest incomes, referred to as the 'minima', in the coming years. According to the PvdA, this group should be protected against any decrease in spending power, a promise made in the election manifesto. In the view of the CDA, the new government could go no further than keeping the decrease 'as limited as reasonably possible'. On this issue, an explicit compromise was reached, which stated that the spending power of the minima would decrease by not more than 1 percent each year. This arrangement thus entailed a concession from the PvdA. If other intentions on schedule for the coming period would allow this, the government would give special attention to financial protection of the lowest income group. No clear guarantees were given however. In the arrangement no exact definition of 'minima' was given; the CDA had advocated a narrow definition and the PvdA a broad one.

The intention to maintain the coupling of wages to social benefits was an explicit compromise. This entailed a payoff for the PvdA, although it was not perceived as a really important concession by the CDA. For this reason (and because on other items mostly vague intentions were written down), the CDA appeared to be more satisfied with the results of bargaining over income policy than the PvdA.

Another conflict was over fiscal policy. One element of the conflict concerned the maximum of fiscal provisions for mortgagees in the existing fiscal system. As a conflict over contingencies, this could be settled by an explicit compromise in which the difference was split. Another element concerned the design of a new system in which fiscal facilities would be independent of incomes. The PvdA opposed the introduction of such a system, as it was seen to increase income differences. D66 tended towards the position of the CDA. A substantive implicit compromise was formulated, giving vague intentions that would be made more concrete by the government.

Investment regulation   A final issue within the field of socio-economic policy was the tightening of regulation of investments. This issue was placed on the agenda by the PvdA. In the view of this party, stricter directions for the private sector (especially in the housing sector) were needed. This was expected to stimulate investments and lead to new jobs. Both the CDA and D66 were reluctant to engage in further regulation of this field, and the spokespersons of the CDA demanded that, to avoid that the Social Democrats would develop false hope, the coalition agreement should state clearly that no plans for legislation on this matter existed or were intended. The definitive arrangement on this matter however, provided neither this clarity nor any concrete indications to the contrary. It thus was another substantive implicit compromise.

Nuclear Power Policy

With regard to the issue of nuclear energy, the parties had widely different positions. The CDA preferred to keep the two existing nuclear power stations in operation, and await the results of a national discussion on nuclear energy before taking decisions. In contrast, both D66 and the PvdA demanded that the two existing nuclear plants be closed down, and that no new ones would be built.

A largely procedural implicit compromise was formulated. This was a typical result, in that in the Netherlands, nuclear policy had become a position issue, and agreeing to disagree (and call in the advice of external experts) was an obvious way of political appeasement. This is what happened. It was agreed that a committee of independent experts should study the effects of closing down the two nuclear power stations. This study was to be completed within 6 months. Next, the government would take a position, and present this in parliament. A second implicit compromise was made on new nuclear power stations. Here, it was agreed that the government would not deal with the question during its term in office.

Nuclear Defence Policy

The issue of the deployment of cruise missiles was highly conflictual in the Netherlands. The prenegotiation positions of the PvdA and CDA especially were incompatible. This was mainly because the PvdA rejected deployment of cruise missiles (it was a key issue in the election manifesto, next to the employment plan). The CDA preferred to decide the matter in December 1981, and await the results of disarmament talks between the superpowers in Geneva. D66 rejected deployment of missiles 'in the present circumstances'. This position was an intraparty compromise between those tending towards the PvdA and those preferring to keep all options open.

Before the final arrangement on this issue was written down, many compromises had ended in the waste paper basket. These texts had contained all kinds of complicated clauses, all of them reflecting the lack of genuine agreement on this matter. As Van Agt complained:

> We now have many words, which actually tell us that there is no agreement at all. Let us simply show this by removing all these words and say that we still disagree (quoted in: Dittrich, Cohen & Rutgers, 1983: 52–3; author's translation).

Eventually, the parties reached a procedural implicit compromise. The government first would consult the NATO partners, and then 'determine autonomously when and on which points decision making will take place'. In the parliamentary discussions following after this government decision making, no coalition discipline would be enforced. In other words, the coalition parties would have a free vote.

In the constituent (that is, first) meeting of the government, the PvdA ministers underwrote a letter by Ed van Thijn, a former *informateur* and the new minister of Internal Affairs, which stated that the PvdA would withdraw from the government if the other ministers would support a decision to deploy nuclear missiles.

Secondary Education Reform

Within the field of education, conflict existed between the CDA and the PvdA over secondary education. The PvdA, and to a lesser extent D66 too, was a protagonist of reforms in the secondary education system. In its election manifesto, the PvdA argued in favour of one general and public system of secondary education for the age group 10–14 years. In the view of the Social Democrats, this reform was an important step towards equal opportunities for all. This new system would be more egalitarian than the existing system, in which, in a way similar to Belgium, public and private (religious) schools coexist with constitutionally fixed equal rights. The constitutional rights of private schools date from the historical pact of 1917. This was the point of concern for the Christian Democrats, who wanted to preserve the existing system in which state schools and subsidized private (Christian) schools existed next to each other.

In the coalition agreement, it was stated that the existing system of secondary education would be changed. To this purpose, legislation would be submitted 'as soon as possible'. This legislation would be transitional, and create possibilities of experiments with the new system of secondary education. As the government was to draft a bill, parliament should decide on the matter not later than in the course of 1983. Furthermore, it was stated that the constitutional article on education would be amended, to warrant the financial equality between state (neutral) and private (religious) schools. To this end, the constitutional amendment was to mention clearly that delegation of legislative competencies to local government would be impossible. The parties thus placed the issue on the government agenda, but did not make further commitments. The arrangement thus was a substantive implicit compromise. Table 7.1 gives the results of policy bargaining during government formation.

Table 7.1   Arrangements in Van Agt II coalition agreement

	Type of arrangement			Total
	explicit compromise	procedural impl. comp.	substantive impl. comp.	
Policy field				
budget	2	–	3	5
socio-economic	3	–	3	6
education	–	–	1	1
nuclear power	–	3	–	3
	5	3	7	15

Putting Deals into Practice

Normally, the presentation of a new government in parliament is a matter of routine. There is no formal investiture, and in the Netherlands the prime minister simply reads the government declaration, which is based on the coalition agreement. But things were different in 1981. As we saw, the coalition agreement contained few clear cut deals, and the government faced the problem that it had to say something coherent about those matters left vague in the agreement and on which conflict had not been settled. This led prime minister Van Agt to postpone the presentation of his government in parliament, to one month after the government itself had taken office. That extra time was considered necessary to clarify some of the misty statements.

Thus, some of the key issues in the coalition agreement were placed on the cabinet agenda immediately after it took office. These issues were the employment plan, cuts in expenses, the budget deficit, and nuclear weapons. On most of these issues, the coalition agreement contained implicit compromises. With regard to nuclear weapons, the cabinet agreed on the position it would take at the next meeting of the Nuclear Planning Group of NATO, at the end of 1981. This position was kept secret until presentation of the government declaration. On financial and socio-economic policy, however, the government got into political problems and conflicts that were hard to contain.

Budgetary and Socio-economic Policy

Two central issues were cuts in expenditures and the employment plan. Policy preferences still were highly divergent – even mutually exclusive. With regard to the employment plan, the coalition agreement just stated that such a plan would be developed within four months after the government had taken office. Further bargaining was also necessary on the size of cuts in spending. As the negotiators during government formation, also the ministers facing these problems had different priorities. In the view of PvdA vice prime minister Joop den Uyl, the government should take immediate action on unemployment, and begin with the public sector. But his colleagues from the CDA and D66 argued that more time was needed for the elaboration of the employment plan, and that the private sector should be given more emphasis. The minister of Finance further increased dissensus by demanding more cuts in the coming period than mentioned in the coalition agreement.

Conflict also resurfaced on the budget deficit. The 1 percent decrease for 1982 mentioned in the coalition agreement was not called into question, but the trouble was that the target remained unclear. The minister of Finance (CDA) calculated that the deficit should be reduced to 6.5 percent in 1982, but his colleague of Social Affairs & Employment (PvdA) mentioned 7 percent. In early October, the cabinet agreed that the government would aim at 6.5 percent in 1982, so this entailed a concession from the PvdA.

In early October, the government also reached arrangement on the financial resources for the employment plan: in 1982, 2.6 billion would be spent. Consensus however did not last long, as the next day the minister of Finance spoke of a 'miscalculation', and quasi disappointedly reported that only 300 million was available. The prime minister supported the minister of Finance, and this led to an escalation of the conflict. On 16 October 1981, still before the declaration was presented, the government collapsed.

A government reparation attempt   A paradoxical element in government breakdown was that the ministers had resigned collectively to leave open the possibility of government reparation. None of the coalition parties opted for early elections (the previous elections were only five months ago), and thus the parliamentary leaders and the most prominent ministers engaged in new negotiations in the informal setting of the government formation arena, and chaired by two *informateurs*.

The key points of controversy were listed and the three parties started working on a document that was meant to update and specify the coalition agreement. In early November, prime minister Dries van Agt reported that the government was 'close to reaching agreement'. But what were the points of agreement? The increasing economic problems had led to new proposals for additional cutbacks in social benefits and tax increases. The social democratic idea to make children's allowances proportional to income was mentioned in the new document, but only in general terms. For financing the employment plan, which had obtained symbolic importance, an income tax increase by one percent (a so called 'solidarity levy') was mentioned, but the conditions and timing of its introduction was unclear. Further, the document contained statements of intent on the lowest income groups and on the budget deficit, but without clear targets. In fact, it stated that the aim of the government agreed earlier to bring down the deficit to 6.5 percent, would be difficult to accomplish (HTK, 17000/9: 23–30; Dittrich, Cohen & Rutgers, 1983: 96–102).

Slow motion replay   The restart of the government was on 16 November 1981. The declaration could not longer be postponed, even though many things were still unclear. The declaration contained a procedural arrangement on nuclear weapons on which the government had agreed earlier. No decision on the deployment of cruise missiles would be taken in 1981, and beyond 1981 the procedure mentioned in the coalition agreement would be followed.

The government now faced the difficult task of specifying austerity policy demanded by the CDA and the employment plan for which the Social Democrats were waiting impatiently. Before engaging in discussions on the budget for 1983, the budget for 1982 had to be revised in accordance with the deteriorating economic situation. The minister of Finance mentioned cuts of 4.5 billion in 1982 and 5 billion the next year, and emphasize that the target of reducing the budget deficit to 6.5 percent in 1982 was sacrosanct. This was more than the total size of cutbacks for the entire parliamentary term mentioned in the coalition agreement. Needless to say that this made it even more difficult to flesh out an ambitious employment plan.

All this led the government to postpone presentation of the *Voorjaarsnota*, the white paper preparing the budget. In the extra time, the parties were able to compromise on the size of cuts in 1982 and 1983, and on the target for the deficit, which would be left unchanged in 1982. The government thus deviated from the coalition agreement (a 1 percent decrease in 1982), and also gave up the commitment to 6.5 percent. The consequence was that the tax burden should increase, and this also was a deviation from the coalition agreement. The ostensible wariness of the parties at that time made that these policy decisions were no longer contested.

The draft of the *Voorjaarsnota* mentioned the 'solidarity levy', and the coupling between wages and social benefits also was mentioned, in accordance with the coalition agreement. The 'minima' however would lose 2 percent spending power if no extra measures were taken. The explicit compromise in the coalition agreement mentioned 1 percent. The new policy package made by the government thus involved giving and taking from al parties, but it was extremely vulnerable to disruptions.

The problem of budget cuts and financing the employment plan continued to destabilize the coalition. Also the implicit compromise on investment regulation generated conflict, and implementation stagnated. The issue of fiscal facilities for mortgagees, to be elaborated by the government, was kept away from the policy making agenda. In early May 1982, discussions in parliament on a revision of the Health Insurance Act, another attempt to make cuts in spending possible, were aborted. An alternative consisting of a series of smaller cuts in different fields was proposed by prime minister Van Agt and was voted on in the cabinet on 11 May. CDA and D66 voted for the proposal, but the PvdA voted against and subsequently withdrew from the government. This time, everyone felt that a reparation attempt was useless, and thus the government tendered its resignation.

Secondary Education Reform

Budgetary and socio-economic policy caused coalition collapse, but what about the effects of compromises in other fields? In the field of education, the intention was to begin experimenting with a new type of secondary education, for which special legislation was required. In addition, the constitutional article on education needed to be amended to warrant local government funding of private (religious) schools. In January 1982, the government issued a white paper on experiments with the new education system. Though the government thus started elaborating the substantive implicit compromise on this matter, conflicts on budget cuts and the employment plan were so dominant that the education issue got stuck in the government machinery.

Nuclear Power Policy

The nuclear power issues were potentially destabilizing, and the coalition agreement contained procedures that essentially postponed substantive decisions. On the nuclear power plants, an expert committee would give its opinion, but at the time of government termination, still no expert report was released. Also the agreed procedure on nuclear missiles was followed, and since a link was made with international disarmament talks that were expected to lead to results some time in mid 1982, the coalition explosion risk of this issue was cautiously averted. The absence of conflict on these issues of nuclear power may have been the effect of the procedural implicit compromises, but as with the education reform issue, it is also likely that conflict overload in the field of budgetary policy simply made it impossible to fight over other matters.

Effects of the Coalition Agreement

It will have become clear from the discussion above that failure was more frequent and also politically more important than success. This is shown in table 7.2. The most outstanding effect of the Van Agt II coalition agreement is negative in terms of implementation: policy predetermination hardly occurred – only 3 out of 15 compromises were implemented. At first sight, effects in terms of conflict prevention are less negative (conflicts occurred in 7 out of 15 cases), but the flow of events in the Van Agt II coalition leave little doubt about the actual meaning of this result. Some matters did not generate conflict because that would have been beyond the capacity of the coalition. Issues that led to new conflict did this several times, or even constantly during the short term in office of the government. In other words, conflicts that occurred were fatal, and conflicts that were averted may have been the consequence of procedures in the coalition agreement, but the early end of the government also 'helped' conflict prevention on these matters.

Analyzing effects at the level of different types of compromises, some differences occur that conform to expectations, even though the overall results are rather negative. Table 7.3 summarizes these different effects.

Table 7.2   Effects of Van Agt II coalition agreement

		Implementation		Total
		+	−	
Conflict prevention	+	3	5	8
	−	−	7	7
		3	12	15

Table 7.3   Effects of types of arrangements

	Type of arrangement			Total
	explicit	procedural	implicit	
Effect				
implemented no conflict	1 (so-ec)	2 (nuc)	−	3
not implemented no conflict	2 (bud, so-ec)	1 (nuc)	2 (so-ec, edu)	5
implemented conflict	−	−	−	−
not implemented conflict	2 (bud, so-ec)	−	5 (bud, so-ec)	7
	5	3	7	15

so-ec = socio-economic policy   bud = budgetary policy
edu = education policy   nuc = nuclear power policy

The Streamlining Effect of Explicit Compromises

The expected streamlining effect of explicit compromises was the exception rather than the rule. Only the compromise on coupling wages and social benefits was converted into formal government policy, but even in this case the early end of the government removed the actual substantive effect. The other 4 explicit compromises were not implemented, either with conflict (2 cases) or without conflict (2 cases). This last type of effect occurred with the compromise on fiscal facilities for mortgagees, which was not dealt with before the government terminated. The government deviated from the coalition agreement by increasing the tax burden in 1982 (the explicit compromise had been no such increase). This decision was related to the parties' inability to agree on the size and allocation of cuts in 1982. The two explicit compromises that did lead to conflict and were not implemented were about budgetary politics, and they contributed directly to coalition breakdown.

The Freezing Effect of Procedural Implicit Compromises

Nuclear power policy conflict during government formation had led the parties to agree to disagree, and the ironical effect during the Van Agt II government is that precisely on these matters no new serious conflicts occurred. The early end of the government may have implied the relief for the parties that no substantive decisions on nuclear power plants and cruise missiles needed to be taken – no doubt such decisions would have involved intense controversy. None the less, the procedures were followed, and in this way the coalition in any case managed to avert the issues during its term in office.

The Boomerang Effect of Substantive Implicit Compromises

None of the 7 substantive implicit compromises was implemented, and conflict occurred in 5 cases, all on budgetary and socio-economic policy. Compared to what happened to the other types of compromises, the boomerang effect has occurred in the way expected. The boomerang mostly was about the ideological differences underlying budgetary policy. The issue of secondary education reform rather was suspended due to coalition knock out.

The substantive implicit compromises (employment plan, cutbacks) were the most violently disputed, and in terms of the functions of the coalition agreement the effects are failure. But obviously the perception of failure is a subjective one, particularly during a government coalition such as Van Agt II. To the PvdA led by Joop den Uyl, the narrow basis of support for developing the employment plan meant that the coalition lost a main ground for its existence. But within the CDA, an influential group led by prime minister Van Agt was intransigent during the multiple rounds of policy bargaining because it tended more and more towards a different calculation: if new elections were held, a coalition with the Liberals (VVD) would perhaps be possible again. From this perspective, a government crisis was an opportunity, not a real threat.

Conditions for Enforcement: Explaining Success and Failure

What were the causes of coalition failure? The conditions for enforcing coalition agreements examined in this study are characteristics of the coalition, of the participant parties, the government and the economic situation in which decisions are to be made.

Coalition Size and Reciprocal Control

The coalition contained three parties and the coalition agreement hardly was implemented. The partners in government followed different strategies, through which coalition coherence unravelled. This may suggest that coalition size – the presence of a third party – made a difference in the way assumed. Examination of the eight months of coalition behaviour shows that D66, the party mostly taking a position between CDA and PvdA in the different fields of policy, was mediating and in this way tried to bridge the gaps between the two larger parties. D66 was cautious in taking a very explicit position and hardly took sides in the many conflicts that occurred (as a consequence, it lost its profile: in the elections following after coalition termination it lost 11 of its 17 seats in parliament). Thus, the three party structure does not seem to have accelerated coalition breakdown, but, in this case, rather may have slowed it down – for what this was worth given the short duration of the government. As in the Tindemans V case, the structure of the agenda was such that the policy decisions most desired by one party where the ones most resisted by the other. The incompatibility of monetary and Keynesian policy was manifest constantly, and this made reciprocal control as an enforcement mechanism impossible. Party political conflicts in which the sum of the divergent preferences is constant are the most difficult to resolve, and thus most threatening to coalition life (Andeweg and Timmermans, forthcoming).

Internal Party Unity

Another assumption was that manifest intraparty divisions in the relevant fields hinder implementation of compromises. In the Van Agt II coalition, manifest divisions existed only within the CDA. This party was the result of a merger of three previously separate religious parties in 1980. Programmatic discord between a group advocating a 'truly progressive' policy and a more conservative group influenced party behaviour with respect to the central issues, in particular socio-economic policy and nuclear missiles. This division also had been a source of trouble for the preceding government of CDA ad VVD. In the case of Van Agt II, the coalition agreement had not received full support from the whole parliamentary group.

The analysis of effects of the coalition agreement has shown that interparty dispute was predominant throughout the term in office of the government. Internal heterogeneity did weaken the leadership of the CDA, in particular prime minister Van Agt, and though this was not the most important cause of coalition erosion, it certainly formed an incentive for the prime minister to tender the resignation of the government. The CDA lost a few seats in the elections that followed, and the general feeling was that the party would have steered towards massive defeat had the government remained in office.

Negotiators as Ministers

At the level of the government, the third factor concerns ministerial background as a negotiator in government formation. The assumption was that such a background leads to more faithfulness towards the coalition agreement, and increases the capacity to implement. The Van Agt II government contained negotiators in the relevant fields of policy. The three party leaders had been very prominent in the negotiations, and they also were included in the informal socio-economic cabinet committee, the so called 'pentagon'. In the other fields, ministers were more outsiders. But the results of budgetary and socio-economic policy making do not provide much evidence for the expectation that involvement during government formation facilitates implementation. In fact, in the Van Agt II case rather the reverse was true. The party leaders were completely focused on their own party preferences, and knowlingly polarized coalition policy making. The opaqueness of the substantive implicit compromises may have reinforced this continued party political strife. The budgetary cycle however required that all what was left vague during government formation was turned into concrete decisions. Here, the difference between extra cuts and extra spending appeared impossible to split.

Prime Ministerial Support

As a *formateur*, Dries van Agt had withdrawn from the negotiations on the coalition agreement. Intraparty and interparty tensions had led to this dissension. Once in office, he was barely able to conceal his disapproval of the coalition agreement, and of cooperation with the PvdA. For this reason he was selective in monitoring implementation of the coalition agreement, and he arbitrated least where it was most necessary. The position taken by prime minister Van Agt contributed to coalition failure.

Coalition Governance Arenas

In theory, the polarized situation within the government could have been tempered in informal arenas of conflict management. But in practice, conflict containment was difficult. It was tried already within one month after the Van Agt II government took office, when the government was unable to formulate the declaration to be presented in parliament. But when the coalition agreement was updated and things were made more explicit, interparty tensions continued within the government and the 'pentagon', the informal cabinet committee on budgetary and socio-economic policy. This pentagon contained the party leaders. Contacts between ministers and other sections of the parties were maintained separately within the three parties. If any effect, these contacts induced the relevant ministers to stand firm during negotiations. As Andeweg (1985: 150) has put it, during the Van Agt II government, the socio-economic pentagon became the site of party political war. Thus, in a coalition in which enforcement and conflict management arenas external to the government were most needed, they were not in operation. As a consequence, conflicts not possible to contain within internal cabinet arenas could not be contained at all, and this clearly was fatal.

Economics and Personal Relationships

Both the economic environment and interpersonal relationships were detrimental to coalition life. The economic forecasts on which the coalition agreement was made appeared to be too optimistic. When the consequences of the second international oil crisis became visible, CDA and PvdA insisted even more strongly on their divergent policy preferences. Though the downward economic trend itself was not a cause of coalition collapse, it led to contradictory problem definitions, and as such was an unfavourable condition.

The troubled personal relationship between the two main party leaders Dries van Agt (CDA), prime minister, and Joop den Uyl (PvdA), vice prime minister, was legendary – it certainly reinforced the unwillingness to give way in confrontations.

Given the emphasis on internal arenas for conflict management, there were no means to limit the impact of this factor on coalition life.

Conclusion

The Van Agt II government emerged from a coalition formation process in which party political constraints were important. Due to these constraints, Christian Democrats (CDA) and Social Democrats (PvdA) had no choice but to coalesce, with D66 as a third party. Party political differences between the two largest parties were impossible to bridge, and deals made over policy problems mostly were substantive implicit compromises or procedures. What was written down in the coalition agreement on budgetary policy, socio-economic issues and other matters was mostly a codification of disagreement. Thus the agenda was formulated, but policy decisions had to be made by the government.

The Van Agt II government however became an arena of a war of trenches between the two large parties. If general intentions require a fair amount of goodwill, the story of this coalition was one of interpretation struggles and conflict escalation. Thus the substantive implicit compromises not only had a boomerang effect, as was expected, but policy making became completely paralyzed. The most positive result was that the procedural implicit compromises made on nuclear power policy at least averted conflict on these matters. But controversy over budget cuts and employment plan spending was so dominant that there was hardly any policy making capacity left.

The key factor that frustrated enforcement of the coalition agreement was that policy problems were constructed as ideological confrontations, and the conditions for enforcement considered in this study did not alleviate this. Within an economic environment that produced decreasing government revenues and a rising unemployment, any coalition government faces the need to set priorities. With an emphasis on informal arenas within the government where political and personal antagonism is largest, redistributive conflicts were hard to settle. A prime minister that does not support the coalition agreement nor even the existence of the coalition itself also did not make enforcement easier. Internal party divisions within the CDA may have weakened this party, but the effect was not a stronger position of the PvdA but instead an increased intransigence of the CDA party leader. A number of ministers had participated in government formation, but this yielded no morality of obligation.

Reciprocal control between coalition parties may work as an enforcement mechanism, but the structure of the agenda was such that cooperation in implementing one compromise incurred costs for one party without gains for that party on another subject. This was because increasing the size of cuts in spending, the demand of the CDA, was incompatible to public money transfers to create jobs, the intention to which the PvdA had linked its credibility as a workers' party. With this credibility at stake, and for the CDA the prospect that new elections could lead to a majority for the CDA-VVD combination, the benefits did no longer outweigh the costs of the coalition.

Chapter 8

The Lubbers I Government (1982–86)

Building a Two Party Coalition

After the Van Agt II government broke down in May 1982, elections were held in September 1982, in which not the CDA but the PvdA became the largest party. The VVD also gained seats, and, despite the losses for the CDA, these two parties obtained a parliamentary majority. The CDA however had announced that the largest party should first try to form a government.

Though government formation in the Netherlands is not typically a ritual dance, the attempt to rebuild a coalition of PvdA and CDA certainly was. The CDA was allowed the second bid for partnership, and an alliance with the VVD was established easily. The only thing about the CDA that worried the VVD were its internal divisions. If a coalition of CDA and VVD would be formed, it had a narrow parliamentary majority. Hence, not only coalition discipline but also party discipline would be important.

This strategic concern of the VVD and the CDA's experience during the previous coalition induced both parties to establish unambiguous commitments during government formation. Thus policy divergence was not avoided nor appeased but was given broad attention. Different policy fields were dealt with in two large work groups of party delegates. These work groups scrutinized all points of disagreement and they did this so rigorously and in detail that the formulation of compromises became a problem.

None the less, the coalition agreement was completed and was approved by the parliamentary groups of the CDA and the VVD at the end of October 1982 (HTK, 1982–83, 17555/7). The coalition agreement again was longer and more comprehensive than before (20,300 words). Ostensibly, the parties' commitment to the agreement was so selfevident that this was not mentioned separately in the document, except for a note in one of the parts of the agreement saying that ministers were expected to commit themselves to the contents (HTK, 1982–83, 17555/7: 38).

When also the distribution of cabinet portfolios was settled, the Lubbers I two party government took office on 4 November 1982. The formation of this government led by a Christian Democrat was the shortest since 1967, but the coalition agreement impressed all parties, interest groups, and the media.

Turning Policy Conflicts into Deals

Budgetary and Socio-economic Policy

The summer of 1982 brought heavy weather for the Dutch economy. Unemployment had risen to a postwar record, investments were running back, and the budget deficit had risen to more than 11 percent of the national income. Given this situation, no party denied that a policy of retrenchment was needed in the coming years. When, however, this general point of agreement had to be translated into more specific policy choices, the Christian Democrats and Liberals presented different viewpoints. Manifest conflicts were over the size and distribution of cuts in spending and on income and tax policy. Also the institutional redesign of the Postbank was a source of disagreement.

Cuts in expenses   A first point of disagreement was the size of cuts in government expenses in the next four years. The VVD was most radical, and demanded cuts of 40 billion over the next four years (NRC Handelsblad, 10 October 1982). The CDA found that the Liberals were putting too much emphasis on cutbacks. The only clear intention of the CDA was to decrease the budget deficit by 1 percent each year.

Negotiations resulted in several explicit compromises. To begin with, cuts would be Dfl. 13 billion in 1983, and 7 billion each year in the period 1984–1986. The total size of cuts thus would be 34 billion. This entailed a concession from the VVD. At the same time, however, it was stated this was a scenario to be applied only if annual wage increases were restrained to 2.5 percent. If the social partners were not prepared to restrain wage increases, total cuts in the four year period would be 43 billion: 13 billion in 1983, and 10 billion in each following year. This second scenario benefited the VVD, so that the arrangement contained payoffs for both parties. Thus, the explicit compromise took uncertainty into account.

The distribution of cuts would be as follows: social security and wages public sector 35 percent, health 10 percent, and the other departmental budgets 20 percent. If an annual wage restraint was realized, annual cuts in each of the sectors would be 2 billion, except in the area of health, in which cuts would be 1 billion. Without wage restraint, annual cuts in social security and public sector wages would be 3.5 billion. These cuts were to expected to lead to a decrease in the budget deficit by 1 percent each year, down to 7.5 percent in 1986.

Further, there was an explicit and detailed compromise on cutbacks in departmental budgets for the period 1984–1986. This compromise also contained a qualifier, which was that parts of the cuts listed could be re-allocated, as long as each department would carry out at least 60 percent of the cuts mentioned, and the total size of cuts should not be altered. Spending on public sector wages would be decreased by cutting down on departmental staff, one percent each year, with the exception of the police and the tax office. The government was to allocate the cuts in the other sectors. The agreement only mentioned that to cutbacks in social security would require a revision of the system of social security, and an anti fraud policy. Finally, the parties agreed explicitly to stabilize the tax burden and to decrease taxes for the private sector by between 1.5 and 2 billion annually, and to spend 750 million each year on employment, for example by setting up vocational training projects.

Income and tax policy   The parties disagreed further on income and tax policy. Differences involving party principles, such as the coupling of social benefits to minimum wages and income levelling were problematic. To begin with, the CDA advocated maintenance of the coupling of social benefits to the official minimum wage, whereas in the view of the Liberals the government should be free to decouple if austerity policy required this. Moreover, the VVD argued in favour of a reduction of 5 percent in the minimum wage and social benefits. Though the Christian Democrats also intended to revise the social security system, such drastic decreases of social benefits were rejected as being impossible to sell to the public. A substantive implicit compromise was reached on the coupling issue. It stated that no instrument for reducing spending on social security would be excluded in advance. This meant that the coupling mechanism could be abandoned.

Another controversial point was the levelling of incomes. According to the CDA, incomes above Dfl. 60,000 gross per year could be levelled, but the VVD insisted on a higher cutoff point. This was a point on which the VVD had made electoral promises. As on the previous issue, the parliamentary leaders agreed on a rather vague compromise which said that there were 'limited possibilities' for income levelling, without mentioning whether or not the government would decide to level incomes at all.

A final issue was income tax for double income couples. There were two different approaches. In the first, advocated by the VVD, no difference between couples and individuals would be made. In the other approach, advocated by the CDA, the household income would be considered, and the tax regime for couples would be different (more tax per income). This conflict could only be removed from the negotiation table by formulating a substantive implicit compromise which mentioned that the government was to develop a new system in which both principles could be recognized.

The postbank   A next point of controversy was on the postbank, a new bank for giro money transactions. There was a bill dating from 1976, drafted by a centre-left government. That bill contained an institutional design of a state owned postbank, but it never was discussed in parliament. The Liberals however preferred a postbank with few competencies, limited to the financial services that were provided thus far. In the view of the CDA, the postbank was to become a full competitor to the commercial banks.

A substantive implicit compromise was made, stating that the government would define its position once the Second Chamber had discussed the bill of 1976. In case of delay of parliamentary discussions or if important changes were thought necessary, provisional legislation was to secure a continuation of the existing institutions for money transactions.

Nuclear Arms Policy

The nuclear weapons conflict was left unresolved by the previous government. As pressure from NATO partners increased, the general feeling was that the new government could no longer postpone a decision on the cruise missiles issue. One problem was that the issue divided the CDA. For this reason, it was not immediately obvious that an agreement could be reached easily with the VVD, a party that advocated firmly the deployment of cruise missiles and conformity to NATO policy in general.

A procedural implicit compromise was made, entailing a postponement of the decision on the deployment of cruise missiles, but at the same time the government would begin preparations for the launching site, in order to remain credible to the NATO partners. First, however, the Second Chamber would have 'the opportunity to give its opinion'. This suggested a free vote, but was not made clear (NRC Handelsblad, 4 November 1982). With regard to existing nuclear military tasks, a substantive implicit compromise was made which said that the government would specify its position before the beginning of the new parliamentary year, in September 1983. It was expected that at that time more clarity would exist on the cruise missiles. Until September 1983, the status quo would be maintained with respect to existing nuclear tasks (Nederlandse Staatscourant, 28 October 1982; KHA, 1982: 740).

Media Policy

Fundamental differences between CDA and VVD on television broadcasting existed since the 1960s, when a coalition broke down over this issue. Here, the VVD here was the change oriented party. The Liberals advocated a liberalization of broadcasting policy, to accomplish a 'breakthrough' in the traditional pillarized and noncommercial Dutch system. In the view of the Liberals, commercial broadcasting should be possible at national level as well as on a local and regional basis. The VVD also demanded that foreign commercial stations be given access to the cable network. In contrast, the Christian Democrats defended the traditional broadcasting system, in which the religious pillars (*zuilen*) were represented. The CDA feared that liberalization and plain commercialization would go hand in hand. Foreign commercial broadcasting oriented on the Dutch public was rejected. The three central points of conflict were (1) the admission of foreign television programmes to the Dutch cable network, (2) the possibility of advertizing on local and regional stations, and (3) financing an extension of national television broadcasting.

One possibility for the parties was to simply leave things open. The CDA then could try to form a legislative majority with the PvdA, but that would make the CDA more vulnerable – and the VVD was unlikely to accept such a legislative *amourette* in the first place.

Foreign transmissions   Negotiations on access of foreign television programmes to the Dutch cable network resulted in an explicit compromise. Until the government could present its view on the problem, no foreign programmes with a commercial orientation to the Dutch public would be allowed. The political sensibility of this issue is illustrated by an earlier version of the compromise, containing a ban on all foreign that 'formed a threat to national security, public order and public morality'. This element was dropped upon pressure from the VVD.

Local and regional broadcasting   Another conflict was over the question whether local and regional broadcasting could be financed through advertizing. In the view of the CDA, local broadcasting should be financed through local taxes. The VVD however advocated introduction of local and regional advertizing under the auspices of the Dutch foundation for advertizing in public broadcasting (*STER, Stichting Ether Reclame*).

The coalition agreement contained a substantive implicit compromise which said that 'if regional and local advertizing appear not to be feasible', public resources at a local level should be used, with the possibility of a supplement from the radio and television licence fees that are collected centrally. What exactly was meant by 'not feasible' was left open. This was a provisional arrangement awaiting the government's long term view on this issue.

Extension of national broadcasting   Finally, the parties had different views on financing an extension of national broadcasting time. The points of conflict were, first, the conditions for an increase in broadcasting time for the STER (advertizing), and second, the question whether or not radio and television licence fees should be increased. The CDA advocated such an increase, but the VVD opposed more state intervention in broadcasting. With regard to advertizing through the STER, the Christian Democrats had more strict conditions, such as no advertizing on Sundays and not in interruption to programmes.

Bargaining resulted in yet another substantive implicit compromise: an extension of national broadcasting would 'in principle' be financed exclusively through increased revenues from advertizing under auspices of the STER. The point of ambiguity here was the statement that if revenues from this extended advertizing alone were not sufficient, an increase in licence fees would be considered. Increased revenues from advertising were to be achieved by a gradual increase in air time for the STER. The conditions were those mentioned by the CDA, a concession from the VVD.

Education Policy

A subject inherited from the previous government was secondary education reform. The CDA had many interests in not redesigning the entire system of education, but it also did not want to abort the ongoing experiments with the new school type entailing an intermediate form between primary and secondary education. The VVD however had difficulty with the more 'egalitarian' principles underlying these experiments, and for this reason wanted to keep the scale of experiments as limited as possible.

Two implicit compromises were made. One substantive arrangement mentioned the continuation of experiments, and announced a special bill for financing these experiments. To warrant the (financial) equality of public and private (religious) schools, the constitutional article on education would be amended. This last part of the arrangement was taken from the coalition agreement of the previous government. The second arrangement was a procedural implicit compromise and contained a postponement of a decision on the introduction of the new school type until after the next elections, or in any case until the second half of the 1980s.

Morality Issues: Euthanasia and Equal Treatment

The next issue that divided the prospective coalition parties was euthanasia. The question was whether or not the criminal law should make exceptions and leave euthanasia unsanctioned under certain conditions. The VVD, as the other secular parties, advocated a relaxation in the criminal law, whereas in the view of the CDA, euthanasia should never remain unpunished. The issue was a typical position issue, with the ethical principles held by the parties leaving little room for compromises. The VVD raised the issue to place it on the agenda of the new government.

This was all the Liberals obtained from the negotiations, as the CDA conceded no further than a substantive implicit compromise, which said that the government would take a position after a special commission on euthanasia had released an advisory study. Until the government had defined its position, the status quo would be maintained.

Another morality issue was equal treatment, on which a first draft of a bill was completed in September 1981 by the Van Agt I government (also CDA-VVD). This first draft never was discussed, and focused on the prohibition of sex discrimination (including homosexuality). It was criticized heavily by the religious organizations, because this prohibition implied that religious schools could no longer refuse to employ homosexual teachers with reference to the constitutional freedom of religion. Against this background, the CDA rejected any special legislation, which in its view violated this constitutional right. The CDA suggested a revision of the criminal law on the point of discrimination. The VVD demanded a special antidiscrimination law, and anticipated support from the other secular parties. On this issue, the parties also went no further than a substantive implicit compromise. It stated that the government would reconsider the 1981 bill, and formulate new legislation in which elements from the 1981 bill 'could be' incorporated.

The three types of compromises made in the different fields of policy are given in table 8.1. Though the Lubbers I coalition agreement was considered to be a very detailed document, the table shows that this was less clear with respect to those issues that were controversial during government formation. Explicit compromises were made almost exclusively in the fields of budgetary and socio-economic policy, and most deals in the other policy fields were rather general substantive implicit compromises, few a few procedural arrangements as well. This indicates that the priority in the formation of this coalition was given to austerity policy (on which the CDA and the VVD were most eager to govern together). The other problems were not ignored, but at least during government formation the parties did not predefine policy solutions.

Putting Deals into Practice

To what extent determined the austerity policy package the governmental agenda? How did the parties go about wit the implicit compromises on education, antidiscrimination policy and nuclear missiles?

Table 8.1   Arrangements in Lubbers I coalition agreement

	Type of arrangement			Total
	explicit	procedural	implicit	
Policy field				
budget	6	–	1	7
socio-economic	1	–	5	6
media	1	–	2	3
nuclear weapons	–	1	1	2
education	–	1	1	2
morality	–	–	2	2
	8	2	12	22

Budgetary and Socio-economic Policy

The coalition agreement contained arrangements which indicated or indeed stipulated in detail the size of cutbacks in different sectors over the next four years. Compromises also were made on the ways in which these cuts had to be accomplished, state revenues were to be increased, and all this within the commitment to a decrease in the general tax burden.

Cuts in 1983   The first test of the coalition agreement was the discussions on the *Voorjaarsnota* 1983, the white paper from the minister of Finance giving the financial possibilities and impossibilities for the budgetary year. The budget for 1983 had been made by the previous government, and the minister of Finance declared that the financial situation required more drastic cutbacks in the fields of social benefits, health and public sector wages, so that the budget deficit could be decreased in the way stated in the coalition agreement (Toirkens, 1988: 109). Before these problems occurred, the government had already made some changes in the distribution of cuts in the departmental budgets for 1984. The coalition agreement mentioned the possibility of re-allocating a certain part of the cuts in departmental budgets.

Expectations of new financial problems made the minister of Finance demand 3.5 billion extra cuts in 1983 – the explicit compromise made during government formation mentioned 13 billion as a total for 1983. Agreement was reached on extra cuts of 2 billion and 3.5 billion in 1984. At variance with the coalition agreement, taxes would be increased, which meant that the promised financial relief for the private sector was abandoned (Toirkens, 1988: 111–112). One of the ways of realizing these extra cuts was a decrease in social benefits by 2 percent on 1 October 1983, for which a special bill needed to be drafted. This decision was a specification of the substantive implicit compromise on cutting social benefits.

These developments had consequences for income policy. Conflict broke out over the coupling of social benefits and wages, on which the coalition agreement contained a rather ambiguous implicit compromise. The CDA insisted that the coupling mechanism be maintained, a point on which the VVD gave way, allegedly 'because in this early stage this issue is not worth a government crisis' (KHA, 1983: 275–280, 343–344). As negotiations on public sector wages did not lead to agreement, social benefits could not be cut in the way intended (KHA, 1983: 452–453).

If the *Voorjaarsnota* was about retrenchment policy, the government also discussed employment policy and the effects of retrenchment policy on spending power. With regard to employment policy, a specification was made for the way in which the 750 million mentioned in the coalition agreement had to be spent. With regard to developments in spending power in 1983, the expectation was that those in the middle income category would be the worst off (minus 4 to 5 percent). This implied that the difference between middle and lower incomes would become smaller, which in the view of the VVD was a form of income levelling. During the government formation process, the parties had made an implicit compromise on the issue of income levelling, and conflict recurred at this point (KHA, 1983: 276–280).

During the parliamentary discussions on the *Voorjaarsnota*, conflict on the degree of commitment to the coalition agreement broke out. According to the parliamentary leader of the CDA, the economic problems required that the financial goals be updated, particularly the budget deficit target. His Liberal colleague argued instead that the government should do something about the way to achieve its goals, and increase cutbacks (KHA, 1983: 344).

The 1984 budget   This public dispute about goals mentioned in the agreement was a prelude to cabinet decision making on the 1984 budget. The first move was made by the minister of Finance, who was alarmed by a widening financial gap. This was taken seriously by the prime minister, who proposed extra cuts and an increase taxes and, much against the wishes of the minister of Finance, a less ambitious schedule for reducing the budget deficit. For the prime minister, the coalition agreement was not sacrosanct.

Between May and July 1983, discussions were held within the cabinet and the 'pentagon', the informal cabinet committee on budgetary and socio-economic policy. At stake were the size and allocation of extra cuts, or the extent to which the government could exceed the amounts of cuts mentioned in the coalition agreement. Agreement was reached on 3.8 billion of extra cuts, which would bring the total for 1984 at 10.8 billion. This was much more than the 7 billion mentioned in the coalition agreement. When distributing the extra cuts, the emphasis would be on social security and public sector wages, where cuts were to be realized through cutting social benefits and public sector wages by 3 percent on 1 January 1984. In December, the bill containing this drastic intervention was approved by the coalition majority in parliament.

In figuring out the distribution of cuts over different sectors, the government followed the ratio mentioned in the agreement, at least with respect to the predetermined cuts. The extra cuts were allocated differently. Contrary to the priorities stated in the agreement, more emphasis was given to a decrease in the tax burden, and less to the reduction of the budget deficit in 1984. This last commitment was relaxed – the deficit was expected to decrease only slightly in 1984 (Toirkens, 1988: 113–122; KHA, 1983: 614–617).

In December 1983, a bill containing a new system of income tax for couples with double income was approved in parliament. This bill was initiated by the government, and processed through the governmental machinery without real difficulties. The new system was to take effect on 1 January 1984, and was a compromise between the two different approaches of the coalition partners (the individualism of the VVD and the household principle of the CDA). The bill however was not meant to be definitive, and a number of refinements were planned for the following year (KHA, 1984: 53). Thus far, the implementation the implicit compromise on this issue had been smooth.

The 1985 budget   The discussions over the budget for 1985 however started with conflict over the central goals mentioned in the coalition agreement. Indeed, it was the prime minister himself who proposed a change of priorities. His message was that cuts should be used not only for reducing the budget deficit, but also for decreasing the tax burden. His argument was that public support for policy oriented exclusively to bringing down the budget deficit was waning.

In the first half of 1984, priority setting dominated cabinet discussions. When it became clear that the budget deficit in 1983 would be lower than expected, the government decided that in 1985 there would be a general decrease of taxes for the private sector, a promise made in the coalition agreement. At the same time, there would be extra cuts of 2.4 billion. At the end of August, the government reached agreement on a package consisting of a 0.8 percent reduction of the deficit, and 9.3 billion of cuts, to be allocated mainly between the spending departments (Toirkens, 1988: 122–129). Though no sector was charged less than indicated in the coalition agreement, the allocation of extra cuts differed from the original distribution ratio (KHA, 1985: 38).

In September 1984, a bill containing the intended refinements of the income tax system was submitted in parliament, and conflict broke out. The point of controversy was the size of a personal tax allowance for employees. In the first version of the bill, the government had fixed this allowance at Dfl. 600, but for budgetary reasons this was reduced to Dfl. 425. This decrease was a concession from the VVD. Once accepted, however, the CDA proposed a further decrease to Dfl. 350, and it looked into the direction of the PvdA for legislative support. The VVD however took this issue very seriously, and warned the CDA not to flirt with the PvdA, and even threatened with a coalition crisis. Prime minister Lubbers tried actively to settle the dispute, and in early November the dispute was settled: the allowance was fixed at Dfl. 387,50, so the difference was split literally (KHA, 1984: 774–777, 787–789).

The 1986 budget   Compromising was not as simple on other matters. In early 1985, conflict resurfaced over financial priorities and the size of cuts. As before, the minister of Finance demanded that a decrease of the deficit was the main goal. Other ministers preferred a decrease in the tax burden, and a more limited reduction in the deficit. These two positions were taken along party lines, with the exception of the minister of Finance, who sided with the VVD. In April 1985, a compromise was reached, containing extra cuts of 1 billion for 1986. Cutbacks in social security, public sector wages and health would follow the guidelines mentioned in the coalition agreement. As far as possible, taxes would be decreased, and the budget deficit would be decreased less than the minister of Finance had pressed for. After a few weeks, however, it became clear that this scenario would lead to an increase in the deficit in 1986. This shocked all ministers, and the government promptly decided to make an extra effort to bring the deficit below 8 percent (KHA, 1986: 632).

The cuts or votes dilemma   New parliamentary elections were due in May 1986, and the government faced the question whether or not to continue its policy of severe cuts for the 1987 budget. There were party political arguments for not doing this, but the financial problems were still pressing. An expected decrease in state revenues in 1986 was particularly relevant and once again an increase in the deficit was expected if no new cuts were made.

In the view of the prime minister, the government had to stand firm and decide on cuts before the elections, but the ministers of the VVD had difficulty with such a decision. The Liberals feared that the combination of electoral campaigning and launching another austerity policy operation would displease the voters. The prime minister however convinced the Liberals that there was no escape, and the result was a package of cuts amounting to 5 billion and an increase the tax burden (Toirkens, 1988: 136–141, 164).

When the government reached the end of its term in office, the budget deficit was 7.8 percent. This was close to the agreed percentage of 7.5, so the coalition had achieved one of its central targets (Toirkens, 1988: 176–177). An intention that remained unaccomplished however was a decrease in the size of the civil service by 2 percent per year. Indeed, in 1986, more people were employed in the public sector than in 1982 (ibid).

The postbank   The substantive implicit compromise on the postbank was implemented, and a bill was approved in parliament in June 1985. The bill was based on a compromise in which the new postbank was designed as a private institution with limited competencies.

Nuclear Arms

With regard to nuclear weapons, a procedural arrangement containing a postponement of the decision on cruise missiles and a substantive implicit compromise on existing nuclear military tasks were made in government formation. In June 1983, the government took a decision about locating launching facilities for the cruise missiles. The Defence minister called this a technical decision which followed simply from the coalition agreement. With the exception of three 'dissidents' within the CDA, the coalition parties in parliament endorsed this decision.

In November 1983, the government presented its long term view of defence policy in parliament. This was later than announced in the coalition agreement, which stated that plans would be presented before the beginning of the new parliamentary year, in September. Due to conflict over existing nuclear tasks, only the section on conventional weapons was completed (NRC Handelsblad, 24 June 1983; KHA, 1983: 662–664, 819).

A half year later, on 1 June 1984, the government took a decision on the cruise missiles. The issue had been highly divisive within the CDA, and also between the coalition partners. The decision was a postponement of exactly one year, and deployment of cruise missiles in the Netherlands was made dependent of what the Soviet Union would do in regard to its SS20 missiles. Meanwhile, preparations at the military air basis would be continued, so that, in the case of a positive decision, the building of facilities could be started in January 1986. The existing nuclear tasks would be maintained until 1 January 1986, and then be reconsidered. The decision obtained majority support, but not from the whole coalitions, as 8 members of the CDA did not vote for it. The government decision was saved by the small religious parties in the opposition (KHA, 1984: 369–372).

Controversial as it was within the CDA, the decision gave rise to differences of interpretation. According to prime minister Lubbers, the decision implied that the Netherlands would not deploy missiles if the Soviet Union stopped deploying missiles on 1 June 1984. The leader of the VVD in parliament however declared that in that case (which he thought was highly unlikely) the government still needed to determine its position (KHA, 1984: 436–440).

A year later, on 1 November 1985, the government decided to deploy the cruise missiles in line with its NATO partners. Two of the existing nuclear tasks would be dropped when the actual deployment of cruise missiles had taken place. As a compensation, pressed for by the VVD, conventional defence tasks would be strengthened. This decision was also approved in parliament, but as before, the coalition parties needed the external support of the small religious parties to reach a majority (KHA, 1985: 750–753; 1986: 11).

Media Policy

In mid 1983, the government presented the *Medianota*, a white paper on media policy. This paper was produced without real political difficulties, and this seems to have been mainly because the controversial issues were left vague. Using the *Medianota* as a basis, the government was expected to formulate a new media Act.

Transmissions from abroad In June 1984, the minister of Culture submitted a royal decree on cable television to the Second Chamber. This decree was a specification of a paragraph in the *Medianota* and mentioned the conditions for broadcasting via the Dutch cable network. One of these conditions was that there should be no subtitling of foreign programmes. When the decree was debated in parliament, the VVD pointed at the coalition agreement which was less restrictive, and did not mention the point of subtitling. This view was supported by a parliamentary majority which included the PvdA but excluded the CDA (KHA, 1984: 579–580).

Extension of national broadcasting Conflict on the extension of national broadcasting broke out in the parliamentary discussions on the *Medianota*, which began in the autumn of 1983. The CDA advocated more air time by creating a third noncommercial channel which was supposed to provide cultural and educational programmes. The VVD opposed such a channel with the argument that there was little demand for a new public channel. The coalition agreement contained only general statements on a 'possible' extension of national broadcasting, depending on the financial possibilities. The debates did not lead to substantive results until in March 1984, when the CDA group made an overture to the PvdA; both parties voted for a motion asking the government to consider the possibility of a third channel. Though this was not (yet) a real legislative coalition, the VVD warned the CDA that it would not accept further disloyal behaviour.

In August 1985, the government decided to introduce a third channel, which was done to comply with the wishes of the parliamentary majority. In doing this, the threat (or opportunity) of a legislative coalition between the CDA and VVD was averted. To finance the third channel, advertizing under the auspices of STER, the foundation for advertising in broadcasting, would be further extended. In confirmation to the arrangement in the coalition agreement, licence fees would be increased only if the revenues from this extra advertizing were insufficient. In contradiction to the arrangement, advertizing was allowed between programmes on the existing two national channels. During government formation, the parties had agreed that advertizements would be allowed only immediately before or after news programmes. These decisions preceded submission of a bill on media policy to the Second Chamber in September 1985. When submitting the bill, the minister of Culture said that the coalition parties in parliament should appreciate the bill as a result of long and painstaking discussions within the government (KHA, 1984: 689; 1985: 689–690).

Consensus within the government did not mean however that homogeneity within the coalition at large was assured. Rather the opposite was true. In early 1986, the two coalition parties in the Second Chamber began to question the contents of the bill. The VVD demanded wider possibilities for commercial television, something that was rejected categorically by the Christian Democrats. Conflict also broke out on the point of commercials. The VVD defended the government decision to allow advertizing between programmes, but the CDA referred to the coalition agreement, which excluded this possibility.

Local and regional broadcasting   Local and regional advertizing was the third disputed issue of media policy. The parliamentary group of the VVD argued that the coalition agreement did not exclude advertizing in local and regional broadcasting, but the CDA maintained that the bill on media policy, which excluded this possibility, was a correct interpretation of the agreement. The problem actually revolved around the interpretation of one single word, which could be read in two different ways.

The consequence of this problem of exegesis was that the bill on media policy could not be approved before the parliamentary elections in May 1986. The next opportunity for the parties to continue discussions on the issue would be during the formation of a new government (NRC Handelsblad, 30 January and 12 March 1986; Beleid Beschouwd, February 1986).

Secondary Education Reform

The issue of secondary education reform was placed on the government agenda through a procedural and a substantive implicit compromise in the coalition agreement. Discussions and experiments would be continued, and a bill regulating these matters would be drafted by the government. A definitive decision on the new system would not be taken during this legislative period.

In June 1983, conflict broke out between the minister of Education (CDA) and his Liberal state secretary on the scale of experiments with the new type of school. The coalition agreement stated only that experiments would be continued, without mentioning the number of experiments. In the view of the state secretary, who was supported by the VVD in parliament, the number of experiments was beginning to expand beyond what was reasonable. The minister declared that he was observing the agreement by not taking definitive decisions before the next parliamentary elections (NRC Handelsblad, 24 June 1983; Beleid Beschouwd, July 1983).

In May 1984, the minister reported that legislation would be completed before the end of the year. Due to disagreements on different elements of the bill, however, it was submitted only in July 1985, so a half year later. The bill specified how experiments would be financed and the objection made by the Liberals with regard to the increased scale of experimenting was accommodated by the inclusion of a requirement that each year new experiments needed formal approval of the Second Chamber.

The bill was received by the parliamentary groups with mixed feelings. The CDA was positive, the VVD commented that the government had followed its own interpretation of the agreement (Beleid Beschouwd, September 1985). For this reason, the parliamentary group of the VVD prolonged the discussions on the bill, and in this way prevented that bill was approved before the parliamentary elections in May 1986.

Morality Policy

Euthanasia The special commission on euthanasia that was announced in the coalition agreement released its report in August 1985. It recommended a relaxation of the criminal law under certain conditions. This advice, however, was not the only piece of work on the matter to be considered by the government. In April 1984, a private member's bill was introduced by D66, and the VVD was not inclined to reject this proposal automatically. The parliamentary groups of the coalition parties were as divided as ever in their reactions to the commission's advice and to the bill. At the same time, the views of the VVD and the PvdA were converging, but the CDA ministers declared that they would not accept a legislative alliance between the VVD and opposition parties.

With the two responsible ministers (Health and Justice) belonging to different parties, the party political element in the conflict was also reinforced within the government. At the end of 1985, prime minister Ruud Lubbers stated that legislation on euthanasia should not be expected before the next elections. In January 1986, the government reached agreement on a first draft, which however would be submitted in parliament only if a majority desired legislation. Lubbers himself preferred to shelve the issue. The parliamentary group of the CDA supported the first draft because it was more restrictive than the liberal D66 private member's bill. The VVD preferred the private member's bill. The parliamentary leader of the CDA reacted by complaining that

> the VVD seems to participate in two coalitions. One is the formal coalition with the CDA, in which the country's economic and financial problems are dealt with. The other is an informal coalition with the PvdA and D66 to strike deals on immaterial issues. Euthanasia is just one example (...) In the next coalition agreement firm commitments must be made, for otherwise we do not know where we stand with the VVD (KHA, 1986: 299).

After the prime minister declared that the ministers of the CDA would sooner resign than sign a bill they did not support, the parliamentary leader of the VVD suggested that the matter be postponed. The consequence was that the bill could not be submitted before the elections and a coalition crisis was avoided (KHA, 1986: 296–299, 324–326).

Equal treatment   Halfway its term in office, the government had not reached agreement over a bill regulating equal treatment. There were two main points of controversy between the parties. First, there was the question whether or not constitutional article 1 prohibiting discrimination weighed heavier than the freedom of religion mentioned in a different constitutional article. Second, disagreement existed over what the contents of the new law, in particular with regard to the position of homosexual teachers at religious schools. This lack of results induced the VVD to table a motion in the Second Chamber asking the government to come up with a bill, and thus implement the coalition agreement, before June 1985. This motion was supported by the PvdA and D66, but not by the CDA.

In September 1985, prime minister Lubbers declared publicly that the government had failed to reach agreement on a bill and added that the matter would be a free issue in parliament. The parliamentary groups of the CDA and VVD interpreted this differently. A spokesman from the CDA in the Second Chamber objected that an issue could only be free if this was stated explicitly in the coalition agreement. With antidiscrimination legislation this was not the case, and therefore the parties should observe their commitments. In contrast, the VVD group began to look in the direction of the PvdA and started preparations of a bill. In December 1985, the party presented what was called cautiously a 'first draft of a possible parliamentary initiative'. This first draft extended to all kinds of discrimination. This was, however, an unlucky move, as the PvdA gave priority to legislation on sex discrimination and the CDA was still playing for time. No bill on antidiscrimination was submitted before the end of the government (Beleid Beschouwd, October 1985, January 1986). Thus, on this item of immaterial policy, the implementation of the coalition agreement also got stuck in the parliamentary arena.

Effects of the Coalition Agreement

The overall effects in terms of implementation or nonimplementation and prevention or nonprevention of conflict are given in table 8.2. The coalition agreement was an important element of coalition politics during the Lubbers I government. As Andeweg and Bakema (1994: 64) report, ministers considered it as 'something like a law'. In 1986, the minister of Finance commented that

> next time we should make a coalition agreement that leads less to discussions about the details of arrangements. (...) Sometimes, the agreement was an obstacle for me; colleagues in such cases referred to the text, which had become sacrosanct (Van Tijn & Van Weezel, 1986: 276; author's translation).

These observations fit the performance of the coalition in implementing the agreement, which happened with 14 out of 22 compromises. But less generally acknowledged is that the agreement did not prevented conflict as often as assumed. Only 4 compromises were implemented without conflict, and conflict occurred in 17 of the 22 cases. If ministers called the agreement sacrosanct or something like a law, the findings in this study show that this did not stop them from trying to get better bargains even if this involved conflict. These conflicts were settled, but thus not prevented by the coalition agreement. Mostly, conflict resolution led to implementation of the compromise in its original form, but deviations from the agreement also were made.

Table 8.2   Effects of Lubbers I coalition agreement

		Implementation		Total
		+	−	
Conflict prevention	+	4	1	5
	−	10	7	17
		14	8	22

The Streamlining Effect of Explicit Compromises

To what extent did explicit compromises streamline policy making in the Lubbers I coalition, given that conflict was frequent? As table 8.3 summarizes, there were 8 explicit compromises, mostly on budgetary policy, and only two were implemented without conflict. The distribution of cuts between the major spending areas outlined in the agreement was followed, be it that the allocation of extra cuts was different each year. The one case of nonimplementation without conflict was about the intention to cut civil service personnel by 2 percent each year. This was a measure of which the effects are notoriously difficult to assess, and apparently it also was not monitored as much as the other intentions.

Relatively the most frequent effect was implementation involving conflict (3 out of 8 cases). Here, the compromises were about the size and distribution of cutbacks. Often, the minister of Finance used the coalition agreement to legitimize these cutbacks. Even when compromises were specific and detailed, however, they were not always accepted immediately by all ministers. Decisions on the allocation of cuts among the different spending departments mostly were made in line with the agreement, or were based partly on it, but they also involved conflict. The most striking example is the budget deficit, on which the parties struggled but eventually the target of 7.5 percent was almost reached. which was a subject of Ministers simply tried to limit the pains for their department as much as possible, and for this they were willing to fight. But this was done up to a point, not putting the survival of the coalition at risk. In an analysis of austerity policy making, Toirkens (1988: 143) argues that the Lubbers I coalition agreement reduced mistrust between ministers with regard to cutbacks in departmental budgets, but this seems to be too optimistic about the role of the agreement. This is illustrated further by the effects of 2 explicit compromises, which led to conflict and were not implemented. The promise to freeze the tax burden was not kept, and the arrangement on cable access to foreign programmes remained controversial and implementation foundered because the Liberals delayed the legislative process.

In short, explicit compromises barely streamlined policy making, but since conflict resolution worked ell in this coalition, most of the compromises of this type eventually were implemented, in their original form or after some modifications were made.

Table 8.3   Effects of types of arrangements

	Type of arrangement			Total
	explicit	procedural	implicit	
Effect				
implemented no conflict	2 (bud, so-ec)	1 (edu)	1 (so-ec)	4
not implemented no conflict	1 (bud)	–	–	1
implemented conflict	3 (bud)	1 (nuc)	6 (so-ec, bud, nuc)	10
not implemented conflict	2 (bud, med)	–	5 (med, mor, edu)	7
	8	2	12	22

bud = budgetary policy　　　　so-ec = socio-economic policy
edu = education policy　　　　　nuc = nuclear weapons policy
med = media policy　　　　　　mor = morality policy

The Freezing Effect of Procedural Implicit Compromises

There were two important procedural arrangements. One of these contained a postponement of definitive decisions on secondary education reform, in an attempt to remove this part of the subject from the agenda. This worked. The other arrangement was a postponement of a decision on cruise missiles until a later stage in the government's life, and this procedure was observed but only after some conflict. The aim of this type of arrangement was depoliticization, and this was accomplished in part, not entirely.

The Boomerang Effect of Substantive Implicit Compromises

The occurrence of conflict on 11 out of 12 substantive implicit compromises provides evidence for the assumption that this type of arrangement works as a boomerang. But these arrangements mostly were also implemented, at least in the fields of socio-economic and budgetary policy. In fact, the different effects vary strongly between policy fields. General compromises on financial and socio-economic policy were mostly implemented, but only the arrangement on the postbank was implemented peacefully. In the fields of immaterial policy, effects were less substantive. The arrangement on the existing nuclear military tasks was elaborated, at least in the sense that a substantive decision was taken, a reduction of nuclear tasks in combination with the deployment of cruise missiles, though actual deployment would not be realized during the term of the Lubbers I government. On education, media policy, euthanasia and antidiscrimination policy, the Lubbers I coalition did not produce the decisions announced in the coalition agreement. On these matters, the locus of conflict was not always the government; in the legislative process, the parliamentary groups were in disagreement, and weighing risks against benefits, the choice was made not to push legislation beyond the coalition partner's limit of tolerance. As a consequence, substantive policy decisions were left to the next government.

Conditions for Enforcement: Explaining Success and Failure

In terms of implementation, the effects of the Lubbers I coalition agreement were more mixed than in the previous cases. The Lubbers I government put many deals into practice and reached the end of its constitutional term in office, but still there were compromises of which implementation was not completed before the scheduled elections, four years after the government started.

Coalition Size and Reciprocal Control

The Lubbers I government was a two party coalition. The assumption was that this structural feature strengthens reciprocal control as a mechanism of enforcing the coalition agreement. The emphasis on coalition discipline seems to have been a relevant factor that facilitated implementation of the agreement. Though conflict often recurred, most of the compromises were implemented or were modified in such a way that agreement was re-established. This was particularly the case in the fields of budgetary and socio-economic policy. In the fields of media policy, school policy and morality issues, no legislative (voting) coalitions were formed. Compared to the other cases, there were more possibilities for such legislative coalitions, and the PvdA did its best to pull the VVD into its direction, but in the end the two parties remained loyal. When the possibility of a free vote was at stake, the CDA reacted promptly by saying that this needs to be stated explicitly in the coalition agreement, mentioning the issues. This indeed is the normal rule in the Netherlands (Timmermans and Andeweg, 2000: 384). Such explicit exemptions from coalition discipline were not made in the formation of the Lubbers I government, and in effect no free voting took place. This absence of legislative coalitions may be seen in the light of mutual control.

Internal Party Unity

Internal party divisions can frustrate implementation of agreements reached between parties. Deals may not be supported by some group within one or more coalition parties. Did this kind of internal heterogeneity become manifest within the CDA or VVD during government formation or during the life of the government? With the exception of nuclear weapons policy, the two parties seem to have been fairly homogenous. In any case, the two parties mostly were disciplined when budget cuts were on the agenda – even the departmental struggles between ministers from the same party were kept functional, and did not bring the parties into serious difficulties. In the fields of immaterial policy party values and principles were at stake, but these were mostly a source of trouble between and not within the parties. On the nuclear cruise missiles issue, internal dispute within the CDA induced prime minister Lubbers to decompose the matter as much as possible – by delinking the aspect of building a launching site and the decision on the actual deployment of cruise missiles, and by linking this last decision to the results of international disarmament talks. In fact, due this internal party dissensus within the CDA, the coalition *was* in a minority situation on this issue, as the government depended on the external support from small parties for getting its decisions approved in parliament.

Negotiators as Ministers

The government contained negotiators in the fields of budgetary and socio-economic policy and education. Such experience was assumed to be a favourable condition for enforcement of the coalition agreement. In the socio-economic 'pentagon', containing the prime minister and the four key ministers in the fields of budgetary and socio-economic policy, the minister of Finance (CDA) was the only one who had not been involved in government formation, but there can be little doubt about his faithfulness to the coalition agreement. The agreement was a reference document for the large cuts in departmental spending. The ministers that had to find ways for realizing these cuts were in a more difficult position, but the spirit of 'no nonsense' for which this government has become famous was upheld, and loyalty to the deals was part of this.

But in the fields of immaterial policy, it was more difficult to determine what was sense and what nonsense. Here, ideological diversity between the CDA and the VVD was played out, without the sense of urgency that helped suppress conflict over budgetary policy decisions. With the exception of the minister of Education, the other ministers facing the task of implementing compromises on media policy, nuclear weapons policy, and morality issues had not contributed directly to these compromises in the coalition agreement. Yet this did not mean that they were obstructing the implementation process. As analyzed in this chapter, the production of legislation on euthanasia, equal treatment, education stagnated not only in the government machinery but also in parliament. In other words, the weak enforcement of the coalition agreement in these fields was not only a typical agency problem, but was due also to dissensus among the principals – the parliamentary groups that had drafted and adopted the coalition agreement in the first place. Though negotiators that had not become a minister were in these groups, they often were not the first party spokespersons in conflict management. Thus, the degree of involvement of former negotiators, as a minister or, in this coalition, as a parliamentary spokesperson can be related to the degree of enforcement, and thus is likely to have been relevant to outcomes in the Lubbers I coalition.

Prime Ministerial Support

At the end of his first government, Ruud Lubbers certainly had obtained a reputation as an active prime minister. Examples of prime ministerial influence on the implementation of compromises include both successes and failures. In his prime ministerial role, Lubbers used different methods to reduce centrifugal forces within the government. Ministers were taken aside and confronted with their commitments. The outstanding example of prime ministerial involvement in implementation of the coalition agreement was Lubbers' role in decision making on nuclear arms, an issue which he depoliticized by cutting it carefully into pieces. During government formation, Lubbers already tried to limit the role of parliament – the arena in which his control of coalition politics was likely to be weakest.

In the important fields of budgetary and socio-economic policy, Lubbers sometimes made proposals which went against the coalition agreement. This fits the finding of one author that the prime minister did not always back the minister of Finance, who was committed strongly to the compromises on budgetary policy (Toirkens, 1988: 182–182). Though not all prime ministerial proposals were followed, the changes from one financial priority to another and vice versa may be attributed in part to Lubbers' way of manoeuvring. The role of the prime minister with respect to immaterial issues was more limited, because decisions on these matters depended more heavily on the coalition parties in parliament which were more difficult to control.

Coalition Governance Arenas

As in the Van Agt II government, there was a socio-economic pentagon in the Lubbers I government. Issues in this field were dealt with in this informal committee, but when decision making became tense, the inner cabinet which contained the political top of the coalition was also used as an arena. Another informal committee within the sphere of the cabinet dealt with nuclear weapons policy. It was formed *ad hoc* to involve ministers from the VVD, who had no formal jurisdictions in this field, in decision making, and thus to share responsibilities (Andeweg, 1985: 147).

A committee of ministers and parliamentary leaders meeting at lunch time met weekly on Wednesdays. The political luncheons in this arena of mixed composition were important, but its steering potential was limited. Legislation on broadcasting, secondary education reform, euthanasia and equal treatment could have been accomplished if this committee had been able to control the parliamentary groups of the coalition. In the end, even in informal committees, enforcement of the coalition agreement depends on how each party weighs strategic costs and benefits. None the less, the arenas internal to the cabinet seem to have been conducive to conflict containment and implementation of the coalition agreement. The mixed arena did contain conflict, but not always with policy decisions are a result.

Economics and Personal Relationships

The coalition agreement contained the most ambitious retrenchment programme of the postwar period. The way in which economic indicators were translated to the definition of the problems in these fields did not differ much between the CDA and the VVD. When the minister of Finance cried alarm about the budget deficit, this was taken seriously by the whole team of ministers, even though deciding about solutions often involved departmental struggle. Changes in the emphasis on financial and economic goals in successive years, sometimes in contradiction to the coalition agreement, also were based on the interpretation of economic figures. In short, in contrast to the previous Van Agt II government, the economic situation did not give rise to large ideological divergence between the coalition parties, and this helped the process of implementing the coalition agreement.

Also in sharp contrast to the previous coalition, personal clashes were absent, and this factor does not seem to have been relevant for enforcement. An indicator of the good interpersonal chemistry may be that after the parliamentary elections of 1986, the Lubbers II government was largely the same team of ministers. This had not happened since the 1950s.

Conclusion

In contrast to the Van Agt II government, the Lubbers I government was a first choice coalition. This did not mean however that the two coalition parties, CDA and VVD, were in agreement on all issues. Economic deterioration and experiences with political deadlock in the previous government were an incentive for negotiating a detailed coalition agreement, at least on the points on which the parties felt a sense of urgency.

The results of policy negotiations were 8 explicit and 14 implicit compromises, two of which were procedural. Explicit compromises were made almost exclusively on budgetary and socio-economic policy. The typical result of bargaining on what were called immaterial issues (media policy, secondary education, euthanasia, equal treatment policy) was an implicit compromise, in which divergent party principles and ethical values were appeased. The parties were more successful in accommodating party principles on issues involving a clear material aspect, such as the problem of income tax for double income couples.

Conflict frequently recurred, not only during implementation of substantive implicit compromises, which was expected, but also when explicit compromises were on the government agenda. The Lubbers I coalition agreement thus did not prevent conflict; conflict occurred in 17 of the 22 cases. These conflicts however were far less threatening than the conflicts that emerged during the previous Van Agt II government.

The compromises included in the coalition agreement formed the agenda of the government. In some cases this agenda setting was negative and, through procedural arrangements postponing decisions until after the next parliamentary elections, narrowed the scope of action of the government. But in most cases, the coalition agreement specified intentions, and nearly two thirds of the substantive compromises were implemented. Policy was predetermined most extensively in the fields of budgetary and socio-economic policy, which made ministers speak of the coalition agreement as almost a law and, for the minister of Finance, as a 'paper ally' (Andeweg, 1989: 16–17). In other fields, policy prefiguration was more indicative, and particularly on issues involving ideology or ethical values the coalition did not produce substantive decisions within the term of four years.

A more indirect effect of the coalition agreement was that despite conflict between the parliamentary groups of the CDA and VVD, these groups refrained from forming legislative coalitions with opposition parties. This may be seen in the light of mutual control, which seems to have been strengthened by the relatively small size of the coalition. This feature may also have contributed to implementation of compromises on budgetary and socio-economic policy, from which both coalition parties obtained substantive payoffs.

Apart from coalition size, other conditions for enforcement also played a part. The presence of negotiators in the government is likely to have eased implementation of the financial section of the coalition agreement, but on issues where the parliamentary parties were more prominent, the role of negotiators (who did not become a minister but were members of the parliamentary groups) is less clear. In any case, failure to produce the announced regulation of broadcasting, euthanasia and equal treatment was not prevented. On these matters, the strategic interests of the coalition parties were diverging towards the end of the constitutional term of the government. This divergence was dealt with within the informal coalition committee, but conflict containment appeared to be more important than substantive policy decisions. More successful in both respects were the informal interactions in arenas of coalition governance within the cabinet. In these arenas, the big issues of austerity policy were dealt with, and there, prime minister Ruud Lubbers was able to excercize control. Mostly, he arbitrated between ministers involved in interdepartmental conflict over allocating cuts fixed in the coalition agreement, but he also made proposals for updating points in the coalition agreement. In these attempts, his guidance in interpreting economic figures was also important. Viewpoints of the minister of Finance and colleagues from the spending departments were brought together. Often, the result was that policy intentions were implemented as mentioned in the coalition agreement, but in cases of deviation, conflicts over the alternatives were contained successfully. This is where the Lubbers I coalition government is a story of success. Within the parliamentary arena, where government bills on different subjects of immaterial policy were scrutinized, coalition discipline was more difficult to maintain, and implementation of the coalition agreement foundered. A long lasting government coalition thus does not automatically produce policies in all fields. In fact, policy nonproduction in particular fields even may be the price for long duration.

Chapter 9

The Kok I Government (1994–98)

Building a Three Party Coalition

The parliamentary elections of May 1994 following a two party government of CDA and PvdA were dramatic for both parties, particularly for the CDA, which lost 20 of its 54 seats. The winners were the VVD and D66, and this was to have consequences for the formation of a new coalition. The CDA not only lost in the elections, but also was suffering a leadership crisis. For this reason, the party preferred, at least initially, a background position, and did not join government formation talks (KHA, 1994: 524). For a majority, PvdA and VVD however were too small, and so D66 became the obvious third party at the formation table. For the first time since 1917, a government without the Christian Democrats was formed.

Negotiations however were painstaking. First, the three participant parties differed less in size than before, and this became visible in the claims they made. Second, the combination of PvdA and VVD was not only innovative, it never before was considered viable because of the large policy divergence between Social Democrats and Liberals in the fields of budgetary and socio-economic policy. The VVD also had a conservative wing, which was even more remote from the principles of the Social Democrats. The choice in 1994 was to either ignore these differences in government formation, or try to bridge them by negotiating a comprehensive coalition agreement. Third, D66 was strongly in favour of reform of the system of representative democracy, but the other parties were less inclined to put such matters onto the coalition agenda.

All ambitions and conflicts over budgetary policy, social security, spending on different sectors, and issues of institutional reform were dealt with, and this was done in an increasingly hostile atmosphere. This even led to a situation of deadlock, upon which the leader of the PvdA Wim Kok was instructed by the Queen to put the formation back on track. In this second round, the CDA make one step closer to the negotiation table, but eventually the three parties that had initiated policy negotiations after the elections were also the ones that signed the coalition agreement that was completed on 13 August 1994, more than three months after the elections.

The coalition agreement was comprehensive, but with 16,250 words much shorter than the agreement of the preceding two party government (28,450 words). It was called 'Choices for the future'. The first part of the document contained intentions on employment, social security and income, public health and budgetary and fiscal policy. On these issues most conflicts had emerged during government formation. The second part contained institutional reform, physical infrastructure policy, and school policy. The leading principle formulated in the introduction to the agreement was that the new coalition would re-establish the balance between public regulation and private responsibilities – an ambition in which the different

111

ideological profiles of the coalition parties were visible. For the new coalition, the question was to what extent the agreement would give guidance in this endeavour. The Kok I government took office on 22 August 1994.

Turning Policy Conflicts into Deals

Socio-economic Policy

The PvdA and the VVD both felt a sense of urgency about unemployment, and they considered this to be one of the most pressing problems. But the parties differed on what would be the best solution. Here the classical differences between Social Democratic and Liberal theories became manifest.

Employment   The goal with respect to employment was least difficult to formulate: within the next four years, 350,000 new jobs should be created. The more specific goals and instruments however were the subjects of battle. The VVD wanted to implement a scheme for making savings on social security spending, excluding the elderly. Savings on social security would enable the government to lower taxes, and in the liberal view this would lead to more jobs. By increasing real wages and reducing the number of months that unemployment benefits are received, people also would have a stronger incentive to find a job (KHA, 1994: 309–310). The PvdA however did not want to dismantle the system of social security for which its had struggled so long. Instead, the Social Democrats advocated only small modifications in social security, leaving the system in tact as much as possible, and subsidize jobs in different sectors for people that had difficulty finding employment. D66 tended towards the VVD, but put more emphasis on liberalization of the labour market and less on tightening the regime for social benefits. The party also argued that longer opening hours for shops would benefit employment.

Agreement was reached on three complementary packages of employment policy. One was for stimulating demand for labour, one dealt specifically with creating low paid jobs, and the third was about reintegrating long term unemployed into the labour market.

The first package was an explicit compromise aimed at stimulating job creation in the private sector. The compromise mentioned as instruments the control of wage increases and the reduction of social security premiums to contain the rising costs of labour, infrastructure investments for strengthening the economic structure, and a more flexible regime for labour. The relaxation of rules on opening hours for shops, demanded by D66, was part of this compromise. Another important point was that the government would attempt to reduce the collective burden. On all this, Dfl. 9 billion would be spent in the coming years.

The second package was on low paid jobs, for which the PvdA had pressed. The VVD demanded that the traditional coupling of benefits to wages – a PvdA principle long upheld – be abandoned, as this would be less costly for the state. It was agreed in rather general terms that a partial decoupling would be realized in the next three years. An important point was that the costs of labour just above the minimum wage would be reduced, and that dispensations of compulsory social security premiums would be made in a number of sectors, to stimulate the creation of jobs. In addition, collective labour contracts would be not binding in the category of wages between the official minimum level and the lowest collective contracts. According to the VVD, this relaxation of commitments to centrally fixed wages was an incentive for the private sector to employ more people. These intentions however were general, and the deal thus was a substantive implicit compromise.

The third set of policy instruments was for the target group of long term unemployed. Here, jobs would be created in order to facilitate reintegration into the labour market. The parties reached two compromises. One was a substantive implicit compromise, mentioning that exemptions to the Act on minimum wages (regulating the minimum wage) would be possible in sectors where this could yield more jobs. The other was an explicit compromise containing a plan for the creation of 40,000 jobs, and a budget of Dfl. 1.6 billion. This entailed a major concession from the VVD, which was sceptical of such state initiatives of what it called 'artificial jobs'.

Social Security

Social Security was a major theme relating to socio-economic policy. The scheme for saving on social security proposed by the VVD not only aimed at lower benefits by decoupling them from the level of wages. Also a more drastic reform of social security was advocated, freezing all social benefits, except for the elderly (*Algemene Ouderdomswet*). The PvdA however was, on this subject, the party preferring the status quo. For this reason, social security reform was a thorny problem during coalition formation.

Privatization of social security implementation   One of the focal points of conflict was the scope and the implementation of the Labour Disability Act (Wet op arbeidsongeschiktheid, WAO). The general feeling was that too many people were obtaining labour disability benefits, one reason being that it was easier to bring them under this regime than to fire them. Apart from this size problem, the VVD demanded a clear decision on the introduction of benefit differentiation and privatization in the Labour Disability Act, as well as a package of extra measures to be enforced if no clear results would be accomplished by mid 1995. The PvdA and D66 wanted to maintain the level of the Act.

An explicit compromise was reached, saying that labour disability benefits would be differentiated, and that implementation of the Labour Disability Act would be privatized. The implementation of the Act and the financial risks of disability were to be brought closer to each other, the expected effect of which was that fewer people would be brought under the regime of this Act. Employers would be more responsible for the risks, and have the possibility of contracting special insurance. However, the reformed act still would warrant the existing level and the duration of this type of benefits.

In addition, the parties made an explicit compromise to privatize the implementation of the Temporary Sickness Act (*Ziektewet*). The government hoped that, by carrying through these reforms, the number of benefits would go down, first of all the number of fraud cases. There would be more selection, and also more incentives for getting people back to work.

Tightening social security regulation   The previous government had made plans for reforming the Widows and Orphans Act (*Algemene weduwen en wezenwet*). The three coalition parties however preferred to reconsider the role of the state on this matter. Over time, private insurance for covering financial risks had emerged, and this led to a more fundamental question about the role of the state. The existing bill however was based on a continued central role, and thus the parties agreed to consider drafting a new bill, but did not give details or even a time scheme (KHA, 1994: 594). This was a substantive implicit compromise.

Next, the Unemployment Act (*Werkloosheidswet*) was changed, and here the compromise reached by the parties was explicit. No benefits would be granted in case discharge was voluntary, and more emphasis was put on the obligation to apply for jobs (this point was hardly enforced thus far). Sanctions were also strengthened. The rules for access to this type of benefit also were tightened: the applicant should have an employment record of 26 out of the last 39 weeks, previously this was 26 out of 52 weeks.

Further, the Child Benefit Act (*Algemene Kinderbijslagwet*) was reformed. Benefits no longer would increase after the second child. The so called age table for determining the level of child benefits also was altered, the consequence being that benefits would become lower for children between 6 and 12 years and for the group 12 to 18 years. The benefit for children of 6 years or younger would remain the same. This clearly was an explicit compromise made to cut down on costs.

Finally, in the Social Assistance Act (*Bijstandswet*), more differentiation was introduced, conform to the wishes of the VVD. Singles would receive 50 percent of the minimum wage, single parent families 70 percent, and couples 100 percent. In certain cases, an additional benefit of 20 percent of the minimum wage could be obtained (KHA, 1994: 309–310). This explicit compromise was another example of an attempt to save public money.

Reform of the Elderly Act   Possibly as a reaction to the emergence in parliament of two parties specifically for the elderly, the three parties declared not to alter the level of benefits for this target group. But a reform of the Elderly Act (*Algemene ouderdomswet*) was considered to be a necessary element of the overall reform project of social security. An explicit compromise was made on the introduction of an additional income test, to ensure that the target group of the Elderly Act, the elderly with low incomes, would not become too large. It was agreed also that for couples of which one is under 65 of age, the benefit for the partner of 65 or older would be reduced.

Mid term review of social security reforms   The VVD had pressed most for reform of social security, and this party also was most keen on accomplishing the underlying goals. For this reason, the party demanded that the government consider the results of the implementation of the compromises, some time during its term in office. If such a review would reveal that the goals (reduction of unemployment, extra jobs, save money in the different social benefit programmes) were not reached, then extra measures should be taken. They demanded that in the coalition agreement an explicit reference be made to a year to year revision of the coupling of benefits to wages. The other parties agreed that in the summer of 1996, the social security reforms would be evaluated. This would not only concern effects of decoupling benefits and wages, but 'all quantitative and qualitative effects of the government's policy on social security'. This was an explicit compromise, which thus meant that the coalition agreement contained a broad policy package for a scenario in which, in the mid term review in 1996, the results of reform would appear to be satisfactory. And it contained the commitment that extra efforts would be made to achieve the goals on social security reform. In this second scenario, the PvdA would be committed to cuts in the level of social benefits, and to reducing the duration of these benefits.

Budgetary Policy

Proposals for cuts in departmental expenses varied between the three parties, but agreement was reached on Dfl. 18 billion, which was closest to the position of D66 which was between the VVD and the PvdA. The state budget would be charged with 11 billion, social security would be cut with 5,8 billion, and health care with 1.2 billion. With these cuts, the collective burden could be decreased and money could be re-allocated to other sectors in which new policies were developed. A decrease in the financial deficit of the state was also mentioned.

Cuts in departmental budgets   Given the emphasis during government formation on clear cut and doable intentions in the fields where the parties have most divergent positions, it is not surprising that on the size and allocation of cuts commitments were made in an explicit compromise, which was quite comprehensive.

The cuts in the state budget of 11 billion would be divided into three parts. One, labour conditions for those employed in the public sector would be tightened (1.5 billion). Two, the introduction of efficiency measures in the government machinery was expected to lead to savings of 1.6 billion. Three, cuts amounting to 2.4 billion would be made in state subsidies, such as for students and for house renters. Savings on social security would be found by decoupling benefits from wages in 1995, and by applying the coupling mechanism only partly between 1996 and 1998, with 50 percent on average. This would yield 2.7 billion. The rest was expected to from the expected decrease in the number of benefits for the elderly upon introduction of the extra income test (440 million), from cuts in benefits for widows and widowers (820 million), and from privatizing the implementation of the Temporary Sickness Act (600 million). On health care, an additional 1.2 billion would be saved, based on the prognosis that demand for health care would decrease. This would be the result of a policy of strengthening the role of the doctor as a gatekeeper of the health care system (more restraint in sending patients to specialists), and by introducing fixed contracts for medical specialists.

State deficit and new priority setting   The money saved in the ways mentioned above would be spent first on diminishing the costs of labour (9 billion). Another goal to be achieved by these cuts was the reduction of the financial deficit of the state, from 3.0 percent of GDP in 1994 to 2.9 percent in 1998. This would mean that the criterion for membership set by the European Monetary Union, a state deficit of less than 3.0 percent, was met at the end of the government's term in office. Further, about 3 billion would be spent on new policy priorities, such as warranting the spending power of lowest income groups and the 1.6 billion needed for the plan to create 40,000 new jobs. These points were also laid down in an explicit compromise.

The pressing collective burden A problem inherited from the previous government was a deficit of 5.7 billion in the departmental budgets. The PvdA proposed to allocate this problem carefully among all departments, but according to the VVD this would affect government functioning in a number of traditional fields such as police, justice, defence, and infrastructure. For this reason, the Liberals preferred more severe cuts in social security, a field that the Social Democrats were not prepared to 'dismantle' any further.

On this issue the no real agreement was reached, and the parties made a substantive, and rather vague, implicit compromise. How the 5.7 billion gap would be filled was not made clear, and this meant that the parties would have to resolve this problem in the government arena.

Rewards of economic growth While the previous point was risky, this did not prevent the coalition parties from considering what would be done in case economic growth turned out to be more than the 2 percent per year on which the coalition agreement was based. Again, the VVD insisted on clear arrangements. But since this was considered to be a luxury problem the other parties did not want to commit themselves too much. It was agreed implicitly that the coalition would further reduce the financial deficit of the state (2.7 percent of GDP in 1998 was mentioned, the parties already had committed themselves to 2.9 percent). If still more money would be left, the government would decide how to spend this.

Environment: Ecotax

PvdA and D66 proposed to increase taxes on economic activities that have negative environmental effects. The VVD however feared that this would affect the international competitiveness of the Dutch economy. The parties agreed on a general course of action laid down in a largely procedural implicit compromise, stating that the government would lobby in the arenas of European policy making for an environmental tax at the European level. If this was not successful before 1 January 1996, the Dutch government would introduce a national ecotax on energy, the details of which however were left open. At the same time, it would continue to put pressure on the European institutions to introduce some kind of ecotax, so as the limit the comparative disadvantage for Dutch industry.

Infrastructure

Two main national infrastructure projects were controversial during government formation. One was on a railroad from the port of Rotterdam to the German industrial *Ruhrgebiet*. This project was expected to boost the Rotterdam port activities. The PvdA had supported the decision to construct this railroad (*Betuwelijn*) in the previous government. The party argued that it would stimulate employment in Rotterdam, which was under pressure due to international competition. The plan however was controversial among the general public, because the railroad would cut through an environmentally vulnerable area, the Betuwe. Particularly D66 took this controversy seriously and took a critical position. The VVD also was critical, but more from an economic point of view. The more D66 emphasized that the infrastructure project should include compensations for the environment, the less the VVD was willing to defend it.

The parties made a procedural arrangement on the issue. The government would review, with help of external experts, the existing plans for the railroad. After 6 months, the government would give more clarity on possible feasible alternatives. If no such alternatives would exist, then the government would evaluate the environmental and other external effects of the trajectory, and make a cost-benefit analysis of the whole project. It would consider also the way in which priorities for infrastructure policy should be set.

The other point of controversy was on Schiphol airport. The previous government had created the possibility of building a fifth runway on Schiphol airport. There was strong opposition to this from environmentalists, as well as a number of political parties, because the external effects were expected to be damaging, or very uncertain at best. Schiphol is in the densely populated west of the country. Not only D66 but also the PvdA, a member of the previous government, were hesitant to proceed with the plan to build this runway the way it was planned. The VVD stressed its significance for the national economy, but on this point uncertainty also was high.

The parties agreed to carry on with the current plans of enlargement of Schiphol, but under new and more strict conditions, accommodating concerns about noise and safety. Moreover, the fleshing out of the plans was to be more participatory, with interest groups and stake holders being invited to give their opinion. This agreement thus was more substantive, but it was implicit rather than an explicit compromise.

Institutional Reform

D66 was a party keeping reforms of the system of representative democracy alive, and thus it wanted to place this theme onto the coalition agenda. The referendum was one of the key institutional innovations advocated by this party. The VVD however had a different tradition of democratic theory, less oriented to direct citizen participation, and opposed the introduction of a referendum. The PvdA was least outspoken about this issue. The parties agreed that the government would prepare a draft bill introducing a corrective referendum (a referendum in which the voters can veto a law after its is approved in parliament). To this end, a constitutional revision was necessary. The constitutional procedure is that the constitutional amendment creating the possibility of a referendum needs a simple majority in parliament, but after the next elections, the new parliament must support the bill by a two thirds majority. The arrangement mentioning governmental action did not give details and thus was a substantive implicit compromise.

Another controversial issue was the introduction of city provinces. The previous government had initiated plans to establish city provinces around the seven largest urban areas in the country and divide the city itself into smaller municipalities. This plan was in progress, and the parties agreed at least not to bury it. The VVD however was very sceptical. Thus the commitments made on this issue were as general and implicit as on the referendum, mentioning that this project would have the attention of the government, but not giving details.

Higher Education Reform

One of the most drastic reforms dealt with in government formation was of the higher education system, in particular the rules for subsidization. National and international developments played a part. The international element was that more convergence of domestic systems of higher education was necessary to overcome difficulties of cooperation, exchanges, and the value of diplomas on the European labour market. For this reason, introduction of the Anglo-American system of bachelors and masters was an option taken seriously. In national arenas, the VVD advocated that the regime for student grants be tightened according to the principle of 'less receiving, more borrowing'. D66 and the PvdA were concerned about redistributive justice in a redesigned system, but were prepared to make a compromise.

   The duration of study programmes was to be reduced after introduction of the bachelors-masters structure, with only the best students having access to the masters programme. There was to be a basic grant for every student, to be introduced in 1998. An additional grant would be dependent on the income level of parents and on other income of students. The key element was that a system of credit points would be introduced including a scheme according to which a grant would be converted into a loan if student performance would be below a particular level. These points together formed an explicit compromise.

Table 9.1   Arrangements in Kok I coalition agreement

	Type of arrangement			Total
	explicit	procedural	substantive	
Policy Field				
socio-economic	9	–	3	12
budget	2	–	2	4
environment	–	1	–	1
infrastructure	–	1	1	2
institutional reform	–	–	2	2
higher education	1	–	–	1
	12	2	8	22

Table 9.1 gives the types of arrangements in the Kok I coalition agreement. Explicit compromises are clearly the most frequent, something that makes the Kok I

government different from the other two Dutch governments in this study (where substantive implicit compromises were relatively more frequent). Impressive is the extent to which the parties made explicit compromises on socio-economic policy – with higher education policy the only field in which this type of compromise prevailed. This is interesting, given that in this field the coalition parties were aware of the policy distance between them, and of the political risks of coalescing. On budgetary policy, commitments were less often clear cut, thus leaving more political consensus building to be done by the government. In other fields, negotiations not only were less extensive, but they also resulted in less doable arrangements, or in procedures leaving substantive decisions to be taken by the government at some point during its tenure.

Putting Deals into Practice

The three parties thus had invested in policy agreement where it was expected to be not necessary for a viable government. Employment and marketability were the key concepts used when introducing the new Kok I government, and the basis of the plans pieced together during coalition bargaining. While the parties had announced a new style of governing, more open and less committed to predetermined policies, the need to bridge substantive differences had led them to sacrifice this pretension for building more mutual trust. On some issues, things were left open in the coalition agreement, but this was more the accepted result of disagreement than a deliberate strategy.

Socio-economic Policy

The Kok I government started when the economic tide in the Netherlands was rising. Economic developments were very positive, and the prospects for the near future were even better. This was likely to be a favourable condition for implementing the policy packages in the coalition agreement, many of which mentioned specific goals and instruments. For a coalition containing Social Democrats and Liberals, the difference between allocating extra money and allocating extra cuts is crucial.

Employment   A central slogan of the government was 'work, work and more work'. This ambition was prominent in the coalition agreement, which contained a number of compromises dealing with different aspects of the problem of unemployment and with different target groups. The demand for labour did increase sharply during the four years in office of the government, and the collective burden decreased from 45 percent to 43 percent of GDP. The central goal to create 350,000 jobs was achieved already in 1997, well before the end of the term in office. In 1998, the new job counter stopped at 465,000, and structural unemployment was reduced by 150,000, down to 400,000 (KHA, 1997: 624). Another point on which political difficulties about goals and means remained absent was the mechanism of coupling social benefits to wages. The compromise reached in government formation stated that this coupling would be applied only in part over the years after 1996, but the steady increase in state revenues allowed the government to reapply a 100 percent coupling of benefits to wages. Though the VVD originally did not want this to happen, there were no financial pains and this led the Liberals to make no trouble about this point.

The economic successes were ascribed to the government by the three coalition parties, but not all achievements following from intentions in the coalition agreement were made without conflict. An important part of the government's employment policy was the creation of subsidized jobs for long term unemployed. In 1996, already 20.000 of the 40.000 subsidized jobs would be created. At the end of 1995, a conflict evolved over the budget of 1.6 billion for these jobs. Members of the parliamentary groups of the VVD and D66 proposed to spend money from this budget to pay higher wages to teachers in primary education. The PvdA did not accept this, but the conflict that emerged was contained (KHA, 1995: 668). The explicit compromise on this matter was implemented faithfully during the rest of the government's term, and the target of 40,000 new subsidized jobs was reached.

Another package on which the coalition had reached a compromise, but a more implicit and general one, was the stimulation of demand for low paid labour. To this end, temporary dispensations of the minimum wage would be given in sectors where this would lead to more jobs. This was an intention to which particularly the PvdA had committed itself with reluctance. In 1997, the PvdA minister of Social Affairs and Employment took his chance and sabotaged this intention by applying the dispensation only to singles eligible to 70 percent of the minimum wage. Later, D66 joined forces and even proposed to drop the relevant paragraph in the coalition agreement. The VVD however wanted to observe the coalition agreement, and blocked a policy change with support from the opposition in the Second Chamber of parliament. Thus, on this point, part of the opposition in parliament contributed to enforcement of the coalition agreement, against two of the coalition parties.

Social Security The coalition agreement contained drastic reforms in social security, of which all most all were unambiguous and clear cut. The intention was not to bring down the level of social benefits, but to redesign the system and make it more selective and stimulate the different target groups to become more active and, wherever appropriate, reintegrate people into the labour market. Privatization was another key word that was assumed to have positive effects on the functioning of the system.

Most of the compromises were implemented, but not all without involving conflict. One issue on which the coalition got into trouble was the privatization of the Sickness Act (*Ziektewet*). The conflict management machinery within the cabinet and the arenas containing also prominents from the parliamentary parties worked well in conflict containment, and the result was that also the explicit compromise on this subject was implemented. For the PvdA however loyalty to this part of the coalition agreement had required maximum pressure on the internal party branches. But, as PvdA party leader and prime minister Wim Kok said, 'a deal is a deal' (Trouw, 10 February 1996).

It was hard for the coalition to realize its plans on reforms of the Labour Disability Act (*Wet op arbeidsongeschiktheid*). The explicit compromise stipulating that benefit differentiation would be introduced and that implementation of the Act be privatized came under pressure because the required financial resources were found to be insufficient. Another objection that surfaced was that the incentive structure meant to discourage entry to this social benefit also made it more difficult for people within this system to leave, because employers would not be interested in having them. With a delay in the implementation scheme and after some dispute, the parties reached agreement on how to proceed, and they almost entirely followed the intentions in the coalition agreement.

Most other plans in the coalition agreement for redesigning social security also were realized. The reform of the Widows and Orphans Act (*Algemene weduwen en wezenwet*), on which a substantive implicit compromise was formulated, was implemented already in the course of 1996. The regime was tightened, following the idea of the coalition that individual people have their own financial responsibility and that the state should have a minimal role here. Access to the Unemployment Act (*Werkloosheidswet*) was also restricted, child benefits no longer would increase with the number of children, and a fund for the elderly (following the compromise on the reform of the Elderly Act, *Algemene ouderdomswet*) was created to be used for this expanding target group. The additional income test for which the Elderly Act would be amended however was not implemented. The PvdA wanted to make this change in line with the coalition agreement, but the VVD and D66, pointing at the general maintenance of social benefit levels, did not feel for this operation. They proposed alternative ways to cut in this social benefit, and to intensify anti fraud policy. The parties agreed on an alternative in early 1995, and thus deviated from the coalition agreement (NRC Handelsblad, 8 February 1995).

Budgetary Policy

One of the assumptions on which the coalition agreement was based was an economic growth of 2 percent per year. The real figure however was over 3 percent, and this meant higher state revenues (of which natural gas sales were an important source) which opened up the possibility of allocating extra money. For this scenario the coalition agreement contained a substantive implicit compromise, which said that reducing the financial deficit of the state to 2.7 percent of GDP should have priority, and other ways of using the money would be decided by the government.

When this decision was due, the parties got into conflict. The VVD wanted to use all extra money for further reducing the financial deficit of the state, as this would bring financial relief for the state and allow tax decreases. The Liberals also wanted to ensure entry into the European Monetary Union. The PvdA on the other hand preferred a further decrease of contributions on labour, for this would yield more jobs (KHA, 1995: 668). The conflict could be settled by combining the two alternatives. In fact, while the coalition agreement mentioned a decrease of 9 billion in the costs of taxes and contributions on labour, the real decrease appeared to be 17 billion (KHA, 1997: 621). The financial deficit of the state was brought down to 2.3 percent of GDP.

The coalition agreement also announced a mid term review to be held in the summer of 1996. The explicit compromise on this point stated that the financial results of social security reforms and budget cuts would be assessed, and that the government would decide whether a different scenario should be followed. This review was made, but it led to other conclusions than anticipated during government formation. The emphasis was not on cuts – for there was no need to do this – but on how the social security system could contribute to a more flexible labour market (KHA, 1995: 660). Thus, though the policy evaluation took place in line with the coalition agreement, it had become less relevant.

Environmental Policy: Ecotax

The coalition played with symbols by stating that the government would restore the balance between economic modernization and ecological sustainability. Much public attention was given to these goals, but political controversy was lurking when the parties went beyond words. The coalition agreement contained a procedure for considering introduction of an ecotax, internalizing environmental effects of different types of energy use, and the PvdA was alert on this point. The procedure was that the Dutch government would try to place the ecotax on the European agenda, and introduce this tax in the national system if European agenda setting would have no short term results.

Not surprisingly, the European agenda appeared difficult to influence, and thus the issue had to be dealt with by the Kok I government. But the parties were not in agreement about how this ecotax should be designed. The VVD insisted on a minimal ecotax, repeating the argument that the government should not bring the national industries into a competitive disadvantage. The PvdA had more ambitious intentions, but did not want to put the coalition as risk. This resulted in the introduction of an ecotax in a less drastic form, in which the alleged damaging effects on national industries were avoided by simply excepting them.

Infrastructure

A procedural arrangement was made on the railroad project, and on Schiphol airport the parties had compromized implicitly. The railroad project involved uncertainties and strong controversy, and an attempt at depoliticization was made by asking expert advice before taking decisions. In early 1995 the expert committee recommendation was to build the railroad because it had positive economic effects, and no viable alternative existed. In April 1995, the coalition decided to follow this recommendation and thus proceeded with the Betuwelijn project, including a special budget of 820 million for limiting the negative consequences for the environment as much as possible. This last element was the condition raised by D66 for giving its support (KHA, 1995: 668). Thus, the procedure mentioned in the coalition agreement was followed, and turned out to be effective in averting conflict (at least within the Kok I government).

Political progress on the issue of expansion of Schiphol airport required that the general intentions in the coalition agreement were fleshed out. The agreement was that there would be limits to growth, and in the course of 1995 the parties made this point more concrete. A fifth runway would be built, but not more than 10,000 houses should be within the noise zone, and a night regime until 7 AM was to be observed. Moreover, a maximum number of 44 million passengers per year was fixed (KHA, 1995: 531).

These conditions however were not really points of consensus among the coalition parties. The VVD strongly opposed the restrictions, arguing that they would hinder economic growth in the area. For D66, the restrictions were not tight enough, and the PvdA struggled with the arguments of employment and environmental protection which were difficult to make compatible. Alternatives were considered, for example the building of a new airport on an artificial island in the North Sea, but the government decided to concentrate on expansion of Schiphol. In the course of 1998, the final year of the government, the restrictions made in 1995 were replaced by less tight restrictions pertaining only to the level of noise pollution. The number of flights first was fixed at a maximum of 360,000 per year, but this was relaxed later by allowing 20,000 flights per year extra until 2003 (KHA, 1998: 272). The two infrastructure plans were long term projects, but for the government political accommodation on these points before the parliamentary elections of 1998 was sufficiently important to accept that most of the decisions on conditions and restrictions would need alteration after these elections.

Institutional Reform

The implicit compromise in the coalition agreement stating in general terms that a referendum would be introduced was one of the concessions made by the VVD in exchange for other cookies with a more liberal taste. For D66, the referendum had been a *conditio sine qua non* for government participation. In the first year of the government, a bill was produced, but conflict recurred when the bill was discussed in parliament. The battle was on the concrete specifications of the bill containing the referendum. The VVD wanted to exempt many issues from the referendum, but according to the leader of the parliamentary group of D66, this was an unacceptable attempt to hollow out the institutional reform even before it could take effect. By threatening with a coalition crisis, D66 pressed the VVD to cooperate loyally in the implementation of the coalition agreement. Since a revision of the constitution was necessary for introduction of the referendum, the final word on this matter would follow during the next parliamentary term, when the newly elected parliament was to approve the constitutional revision by a two thirds majority. None the less, D66 did its best to make the bill as inclusive as possible, and the VVD tried to cut off some of the points. This give and take process lasted until in 1997 the bill was approved in parliament. On this issue, the coalition agreement was not very explicit, but even so it appeared to be extremely important for policy making.

According to D66, the introduction of seven city provinces, a new level of government between municipalities and provinces, was another test case for the institutional reform aspirations of the coalition. The substantive implicit compromise however concealed dissensus on this point, and in the agglomerations where the city provinces were to be realized, massive opposition from the population became manifest. This made the government decide to suspend the whole operation.

Higher Education Reform

The final issue on which the coalition parties had tried to predefine policy was a radical reform of the higher education system. This reform entailed changes in the system of grants and in the structure of programmes (introduction of the bachelors-masters system). These reforms were considered necessary to cut 500 million in the departmental budget.

However, already during the first months of the government it turned out to be an illusion that these reforms would yield 500 million. In November 1994, most of the points of the explicit compromise were withdrawn, including the plans to introduce a bachelor-master programme. As an alternative, the government, with the support of the parliamentary parties, decided to reduce the size of cuts on higher education to 300 million, and raise tuition fees as from September 1996. The only intention that was implemented in original form was the tightening of the incentive structure in the system of student grants. Thus, this was the only issue on which the coalition agreement was largely left unimplemented.

Effects of the Coalition Agreement

Not in all fields the intentions from the coalition agreement were carried out, but it is clear that in most cases the Kok I government and the coalition majority in parliament adopted policy decisions in line with the agreement. In fact, in no other coalition government analyzed in this book was the degree of success so high: 19 out of 22 arrangements were implemented. Conflicts could not be prevented (conflict recurred in 11 of the 22 cases), but the decision making arenas within the coalition certainly were not battlefields. Table 9.2 summarizes the overall findings.

The Streamlining Effect of Explicit Compromises

Given the success of the Kok I government in implementing the coalition agreement, a more specific question is whether this success relates to the large proportion of explicit compromises in the agreement. The assumption in this book was that explicit compromises streamline decision making, so are implemented without conflict. Analysis of the results given in table 9.3 shows that this was true for most explicit compromises (7 out of 12) (and also more often than in the other governments considered in this study). Another 3 explicit compromises also were implemented, but only after conflict was settled.

The main field where these successes occurred was socio-economic policy, on which the coalition agreement appeared to be a very important element of coalition governance. The political investments made by the coalition parties during government formation to establish agreement on matters involving historical divisions thus seem to have paid off. A favourable condition was the economic growth experienced during this parliamentary term, which reduced the pains of concessions for all parties because the number of hard choices for the coalition in this field could remain limited. Conflicts were not prevented by the compromises on reforms of the Labour Disability Act and the Temporary Sickness Act. These were significant parts of the system of social security on which the PvdA was feeling the social opposition to the drastic changes, and thus the pains of the concessions made during government formation. These reforms eventually were carried out, but conflict on the Elderly Act resulted in the suspension of this part of the coalition agreement. Also the intended changes in the system of higher education were largely left unimplemented, but this was not due to coalition conflict but because of opposition from stakeholders within society. None the less, the effects of explicit compromises were mostly in the expected direction.

The Freezing Effect of Procedural Implicit Compromises

The two procedural arrangements that were made in government formation were both carried out but both also involved conflict. One conclusion is thus that they did not effectively reduce the heat of policy dispute among the coalition partners. The procedures were made on issues involving a trade off between economic growth and environmental protection. One issue was the introduction of an ecotax, the other about constructing of a railroad cutting across a unique ecosystem. In both cases, government decision making was made dependent on external actors, in one case the European Union members, in the other a national expert committee. But also in both cases, the key decisions were to be taken by the government itself, and at that point the symbolic language used in the coalition agreement and in the government declaration needed to be translated into concrete priorities. This was difficult, because the PvdA and the VVD were often pulling into different directions. The conflict resolution capacity in the different arenas of coalition governance was sufficient to contain these problems.

Table 9.2   Effects of Kok I coalition agreement

		Implementation		Total
		+	−	
conflict prevention	+	10	1	11
	−	9	2	11
		19	3	22

The Boomerang Effect of Substantive Implicit Compromises

Finally, had substantive and often vague implicit compromises a boomerang effect during the Kok I government? The expectation was that this type of arrangement involves most conflict, and is implemented less often than the other arrangements.

With respect to implementation, the effects during the Kok I government were more positive than assumed. Of the 8 general implicit compromises that had been formulated, 7 were implemented at some point between September 1994 and May 1998. So, in relative terms, there is no difference with explicit compromises in the rate of implementation. Conflict however was more frequent, and there was also a difference in the relative proportion of peacefully implemented compromises (3 out of 8, against 7 out of 12). Elaborating general and sometimes contradictory intentions thus was more difficult than taking decisions that were already precooked. These less specific compromises were made on socio-economic and

Table 9.3   Effects of types of arrangements

	Type of arrangement			Total
	explicit	procedural	implicit	
Effect				
implemented no confict	7 (so-ec, bud)	–	3 (so-ec, bud)	10
not implemented no conflict	1 (edu)	–	–	1
implemented conflict	3 (so-ec)	2 (env, inf)	4 (so-ec, bud, inf, ins)	9
not implemented conflict	1 (so-ec)	–	1 (ins)	2
	12	2	8	22

so-ec = socio-economic policy   bud = budgetary policy
env = environmental policy   inf = infrastructure
ins = institutional reform   edu = education policy

budgetary policy, but also on institutional reform and infrastructure (Schiphol airport). On these last issues, there was less common sense of urgency, and the parties were less willing to give way on their principles. Particularly D66 needed to engage in brinkmanship in order to have the VVD cooperate in implementing the coalition agreement – the referendum almost was lost. These were also the points for which the economic boom, creating more value for everyone in the coalition, was least relevant. But despite the higher political transaction costs of implementation, also this type of arrangement led to substantive policy results in the Kok I government coalition.

Conditions for Enforcement: Explaining Success and Failure

The Kok I government coalition implemented the vast majority of compromises made on issues that were controversial during government formation, and new conflicts were contained. Explicit compromises were most effective in this respect, as they were enforced relatively peacefully. One condition that already appeared to be important is the economic situation, which enabled the three coalition parties to pursue different policies at the same time and avoid hard choices. As we saw, the Van Agt II government collapsed over such choices in 1982. The Kok I government was able to launch a major reform of the social security system without making drastic cutbacks that would have put the coalition under pressure. Economics thus was important. What was the relevance of other factors for enforcement?

Coalition Size and Reciprocal Control

The assumption that a coalition larger than two parties is more likely to stumble over implementation of the coalition agreement does not find much evidence in the Kok I case. In the three party coalition, reciprocal control was a strong enforcement mechanism. This seems to have been related less to the size of the coalition than to the structure of the agenda set during government formation. The fields of budgetary and socio-economic policy were important to all parties and contained relatively balanced payoffs and concessions. But in the other fields, policy intentions were desired strongly by one party and resisted (and thus accepted reluctantly) by another. This was the situation with institutional reforms, infrastructure issues, ecotax and to an extent higher education reform as well. The compromises made on these matters resulted from a process of logrolling. These issues were not tangential in the sense discussed earlier in this book, in that they did not leave some parties indifferent.

Here, the differences between policy making during government formation and government life come into play. In government formation, the variation in party preferences in different fields was accommodated by linking issues and put them all together into the coalition agreement. This was a process of intense negotiations that took, in the kok I case, three months. Even if this was longer than in coalition formations in the 1980s (it was the longest since 1977), it is still much more compressed than the four years available to a government. But not all compromises in the coalition agreement can be implemented simultaneously, and this is where the patience and loyalty of coalition parties are put to the test, and thus where reciprocal control is a mechanism of enforcement. In the Kok I government, the reciprocal nature of commitments was not only implicit, but also was referred to frequently. Consider for example the implementation of the referendum compromise. When the government had drafted a bill, as indicated in the coalition agreement, the parliamentary group of the VVD started to make trouble and demanded 'compensations'. D66 reacted by saying:

> If the VVD cooperates on this issue, my party will do the same on other policies included in the coalition agreement. But the more the VVD questions elements of the agreement, the less we will cooperate in realizing the compensations (quoted in Timmermans and Andeweg, 2000: 356).

As reported, the conflict on this matter was settled and the compromise was implemented. The spokesperson from the VVD said that the loyalty of his party was not because it liked the bill but 'had everything to do with the coalition agreement' (ibid.). This example reflects the general spirit in the coalition, of which many were sceptical at the outset because it contained parties with fundamentally different ideologies and policy principles. This was the paradox about the Kok I coalition.

Internal Party Unity

Internal party divisions existed in the Kok I coalition, and they made enforcement of a number of compromises more difficult. Within the PvdA, part of the reforms in social security, in particular the privatization of the Temporary Sickness Act, were considered painful because of the negative effects for the most vulnerable social groups. On these matters, intraparty discipline was enforced by the party leadership, in particular by Wim Kok in his dual role of prime minister and PvdA party leader.

Not an internal party division but with an effect on enforcement was the position taken by the parliamentary leader of the VVD, Frits Bolkestein, who frequently challenged the government on intentions not supported wholeheartedly by his party. This certainly increased suspense on matters such as reform of the Elderly Act, the referendum, and higher education. It also was an intelligent electoral strategy; in the parliamentary elections of 1998, the VVD obtained more seats than ever before. The confrontations led to delay in implementation, and also contributed to the nonimplementation of a number of compromises, particularly on higher education, city provinces and the introduction of an additional income test for the elderly.

Negotiators as Ministers

VVD parliamentary leader Frits Bolkestein had been a negotiator, but used the inside information obtained in government formation for his own strategy of challenging the government in the legislative arena. The other party leaders became a minister, and a number of prominents from the parliamentary groups also took a seat in the cabinet. Bolkestein thus did not experience the norms and small group pressures within the cabinet. The distance from this decision making institution is likely to have enabled him to oppose some of the coalition plans, and this seems to have contributed to the nonimplementation of these plans when scrutinized in parliament.

In contrast, the negotiators that became a minister took their share in implementing the compromises on institutional reform (for which a VVD minister was responsible), transport infrastructure (VVD minister), and, importantly, the redesign of the social security system (PvdA minister). The ministers of Economic Affairs (D66) and Finance (VVD) had a different background, but in these fields the favourable economic conditions made implementation of the coalition agreement less difficult. All this suggests that participation in the government of negotiators made a difference to implementation of the coalition agreement. The least implemented compromises were those on which the parliamentary leader of the VVD had most influence.

Prime Ministerial Support

With the risk of alienating himself from the Social Democratic party rank and file, prime minister Wim Kok monitored the implementation of the coalition agreement in all fields of policy. He acted as an arbitrator when conflict occurred, and particularly in the fields of budgetary and socio-economic policy, put ministers as well as the parliamentary parties back on the track of the coalition agreement. Where more leeway for policies beyond the agreement existed, the prime minister often constrained the claims made by spending ministers by supporting the minister of Finance in his conditions (budgetary discipline). Given the political costs for his own party of many of the reforms in social security, the role adopted by Wim Kok was clearly one of a guardian of the coalition agreement and arbitrator in conflicts.

This did benefit his party however in the next elections of 1998, when the PvdA gained seats and strengthened its position as the largest party.

Coalition Governance Arenas

Though in the run up to the Kok I government, many promises were made about a change in the existing culture of invisible politics, informal arenas and secret political deals continued to be important. This underscores the significance of such arenas, and both internal cabinet arenas and sites of mixed composition for conflict resolution and maintaining coalition discipline were used between 1994 and 1998.

To begin with, the socio-economic ministerial pentagon of the 1980s was extended to a 'hexagon', including the minister of Finance. This hexagon was the site where the largest budget cuts and social security reforms were discussed. It was also a venue for the minister of Finance to enforce budget discipline. The inner cabinet containing the vice prime ministers as party leaders in the government dealt also with issues of immaterial policy, on which mostly procedural and substantive implicit compromises had been made. These compromises needed to be fleshed out, with a key role for the party leaders (who all had been a negotiator).

An important part of the coalition apparatus were also the 'turret consultations' involving the prime minister, the two vice prime ministers and the three leaders of the parliamentary groups. Though the locus of these meetings was clear (the prime minister's office, called the turret), discussions often were hocus pocus even to the parliamentary backbenchers of the coalition parties. The turret meetings often functioned to strengthen the collective responsibility for coalition policy. One participant reported about the common spirit: 'It is a kind of follow up on government formation, and real negotiations take place. But the coalition agreement serves as the big stick; if we cannot agree, the coalition agreement remains fully in force' (quoted in Timmermans and Andeweg, 2000: 384). In short, arenas for coalition governance were important for ironing out differences over implementation of the coalition agreement.

Economics and Personal Relationships

Though the prolongation in office of the Kok government after the elections of 1998 involved a cabinet reshuffle, this was not done because of relational problems between ministers. Probably the most outstanding feature of the Kok I coalition in this respect was the position of VVD parliamentary leader Bolkestein *vis à vis* the government, which often led to tense situations. But the rhetoric and the real conflicts that emerged were functional, not personal.

More significant for coalition dynamics, and for success, was the upward economic trend, which yielded far higher state revenues than anticipated during government formation, and enlarged the possibilities for reaching different goals at the same time. This affluence thus made it easier for the coalition to accomplish the targets for creating employment and reducing the financial state deficit, and the revisions of social security legislation needed to involve less cuts in benefits. Though conflict occurred on how the extra money should be spent, this conflict was contained within the coalition machinery.

Conclusion

When the agreed mid term review of coalition policy performance was due, the parliamentary leader of the VVD Frits Bolkestein suggested to write a new coalition agreement. In his opinion, most of the goals mentioned in the agreement already were accomplished (NRC Handelsblad, 22 February 1996). This suggestion was in part rhetorical, but it also indicates that implementation of the coalition agreement was taken seriously by the government. Bolkestein also may have made this point because the intentions not yet implemented at mid term were the ones least wanted by the VVD. Whatever the motivation, the coalition partners firmly rejected the idea, and called upon the responsibility of the VVD to remain loyal.

The coalition agreement made in the summer of 1994 bridged differences between two traditional rival parties, the PvdA and the VVD, and this was done by formulating explicit compromises on issues where controversy (and the risk of conflict during government life) was largest. Thus in the fields of budgetary and socio-economic policy, the government commenced its term in office with clear commitments. Things were settled less in detail in other policy fields, such as institutional reform, infrastructure, and the environment. For D66, the third and smallest coalition member, attention for a number of its desideratums was a condition for participation, and the other parties allowed these matters to be placed onto the agenda. Absent from the coalition agenda set in government formation were ethical problems such as euthanasia, rights for homosexuals, assisted reproduction, etc. – matters that usually involved conflict and anxiety in previous government formations including the Christian Democrats. These subjects were less controversial among the three secular parties which now had a majority enabling them to liberalize existing regulation, but the Kok I coalition kept these matters at a low profile.

Given the priorities set in the coalition agreement, the government set course for drastic reforms of social security and the creation of jobs. Economic growth was much stronger than anticipated, and this helped accomplishing the goals incorporated into explicit compromises within four years. The opposition led by the CDA wondered whether it really was government policy that made the difference, but in the parliamentary elections of 1998, the voters rewarded the Kok I government by giving it a larger majority and a second term in office.

The positive substantive effects of the coalition agreement, with an implementation ratio of 19/22, underline the significance of this document between 1994 and 1998. Conflicts that recurred, were contained in the internal cabinet arenas or in the mixed arena containing ministers and parliamentary leaders. Ministerial background as a negotiator and the arbitrating role of the prime minister also seem to have been conducive to enforcement of the coalition agreement whenever individual ministers or members of the parliamentary groups started to make trouble. Policy decisions on institutional reform and infrastructure however were delayed in the parliamentary arena, where coalition discipline depends strongly on the degree of intraparty discipline. The parliamentary leader of the VVD was not always willing to enforce party discipline on issues containing concessions, but the insistence of the other coalition parties worked to maintain loyalty.

These types of dynamics during the Kok I government are evidence that the politics of making and enforcing coalition agreements has institutionalized in the Dutch system. Before and even during the formation of the Kok I coalition, the parties announced a change in the style of policy making, but this did not happen at all. The coalition agreement was shorter than the previous one, but enforcement of the agreement was organized in the same ways as before, with even more emphasis on reciprocal control, and the informal arenas of conflict management continued to be central in keeping the coalition on the track. This case study illustrates that the politics of accommodation in the Netherlands remained in tact, even during a coalition that was built to produce political innovations.

Chapter 10

The High Politics of Coalition Agreements

Introduction

In this study, the functions and effects of coalition agreements have been assessed to learn more about what coalition governments do. Party leaders and the delegations they bring along to the government formation table invest time in writing coalition agreements, and they do this because they expect beneficial effects – more efficiency in coalition policy making, and more peace in the government. Written coalition agreements are considered to reduce uncertainty and mistrust, and this is why they have institutionalized in countries with coalition governments.

Given this alleged role of coalition agreements in maintaining coalition governments, the key questions in this book are whether these documents do prevent conflict and make policy making easier by providing deals than can be implemented. These questions are examined for cases taken from Belgium and the Netherlands, two countries where, since the mid 1960s, comprehensive and detailed coalition agreements are formulated and published.

Coalition agreements establish a relationship between parties taking office together. Though parties may not really discuss all matters that are within the scope of government action, negotiations on a coalition agreement are more than just windrow dressing. Party leaders may give attention to particular subjects because this is what they are expected to do. Party enthusiasts and followers expect that party ideology and principles are the input of government formation. Voters and the general public expect prominents to discuss the problems of the country. But beyond the rhetoric and symbolic intentions, political parties deal also with issues that are salient and divide them. On these matters, coalition agreements are ascribed the substantive functions of providing an agenda and preventing the recurrence of conflict during the life of the government. With these functions in mind, parties engage in extensive negotiations in government formation because this provides an 'institutionalized extrainstitutional arena' of invisible politics (Peterson and De Ridder, 1986). During government formation, parties can link issues and make packages of policy commitments.

As said, party leaders do not negotiate everything. If they emphasize different subjects, such tangential preferences can be listed. What parties usually do given the informal but pressing time constraint on government formation, is focus on divergent preferences – on issues that divide them. These issues may change from election to election and from coalition to coalition, though some are more permanent, particularly issues in the fields of budgetary and socio-economic policy. The stakes of parties in these fields are high, because voters punish or reward them for their performance. Conflicts on budgets and socio-economic policies are often manifest, as developments in the economic environment may require that governments set priorities and make hard choices. Unfavourable economic conditions in the 1970s and 1980s mandated that the parties made such hard choices in the annual budgetary cycle.

Controversial issues are important in government formation, and they have formed the point of departure in the case studies in this book. Policy conflicts were turned into more or less specific deals. Explicit compromises contain clear commitments on policy contents, substantive implicit compromises are general or even ambiguous and need further elaboration, and procedural implicit compromises indicate the ways in which the parties should deal with the issue. The case studies have shown what type of arrangement was made on what issues. Typically, on matters involving party principles that are difficult to make compatible, implicit compromises were made. These matters included morality issues such as abortion, euthanasia, and equal treatment of homosexuals. Explicit compromises were frequent in the fields of budgetary and socio-economic policy, where differences appeared more easy to split.

The second step in the analysis moved from the types of arrangements to their effects during coalition life. The effects of coalition agreements on coalition peace and policy may differ according to the types of compromises. In this way, the assessment of the functions of agreements may show the variation that exists in the real world of coalition politics. The cases have shown that the distinction between types of arrangements is useful for empirical analysis of coalition agreements, and they differ in their effects during coalition life.

In this final chapter, the broader patterns in the findings from the five case studies are considered. The same analytical steps as in the case studies, one from conflicts to deals, and two from deals to effects, is followed. What patterns emerge in the types of arrangements made during government formation, and in the effects on coalition policy making and conflict management? And what is the leverage of the different conditions for enforcement of coalition agreements? The emphasis in this chapter is not on comparing the case studies per se, but on the general empirical patterns that emerge. The central aim of this study is to explore the politics of making and enforcing coalition agreements.

Policy Conflicts and Political Deals

Agenda Setting in Government Formation

The issues debated during the government formations of 1973 and 1977 in Belgium, and 1981, 1982 and 1994 in the Netherlands included some conflicts inherited from the previous coalition. Most however were 'new' conflicts which occurred when party policy positions from election manifestos were confronted. Only the formation of the Leburton government in Belgium in 1973 was not preceded by parliamentary elections, and the issue that triggered the collapse of the previous government (the rights of French and Dutch language minorities in different parts of the country) was prominent on the formation agenda. The Lubbers I government in the Netherlands in

1982 inherited a massive budgetary problem from the Van Agt II government, which had ended early in party political deadlock. Issues that were not left by the outgoing government as points of battle often also were themes over which coalition parties experienced repeated conflict. In part, this is because parties have identities that require them to profile themselves on particular matters salient to all, and the increasing electoral competition is a driving force for keeping distinct policy profiles alive.

In the two Belgian cases and in the Lubbers I coalition, the pursuit of policy on salient but controversial issues formed the *raison d'être* of the government. The Leburton government and the Tindemans V government both were coalitions controlling more than two thirds of the seats in parliament to ensure in advance the constitutionally required qualified majority for regionalization. Disputes over language and regionalization mostly were turned into explicit compromises. The Lubbers I coalition was formed in a conscious move of the Christian Democrats to pursue a policy of economic retrenchment, after the previous government with the PvdA and D66 ended in political chaos.

Two important fields in which parties thus did not ignore but focused on policy divergence were budgetary and socio-economic policy and regionalization. Other matters on the agenda often related to the old religious cleavage, the division between religious and secular parties which dates back to the period in which the traditional political parties were established. On education policy, on which in Belgium and the Netherlands historical pacts between secular and religious parties exist, deals were sometimes explicit, but more often implicit. The religious-secular divide also played a part in ethical questions and media policy. Media issues, in particular on broadcasting, were sensitive because as in the field of education, the Belgian and Dutch systems consist of different organizations (the famous 'pillars') that coexist and have their own traditional social and denominational clientele. The Christian Democrats displayed great suspicion towards proposals affecting the traditional institutional arrangements in these fields. Such proposals however were made by other parties because the traditional segmented organizations were losing their social basis and the national system was seen to need more openness.

Finally, policy fields in which conflicts occurred were nuclear power, infrastructure, and the environment. In the early 1980s, nuclear policy, especially in the military sphere, ceased to be a field of consensus among the political parties in the Netherlands. In two governments, issues in this area divided the coalition parties, and also internally divided one party, the CDA. Infrastructure projects and environmental policy were disputed in the Kok I coalition, formed in 1994. Environmental issues became more salient in politics in the late 1980s in Western Europe.

The relevant policy fields and the types of compromises made in the five coalition governments are summarized in table 10.1. The typical 'Belgian' issues are given in the upper part of the table, the issues salient only in one of more Dutch coalitions are listed in the lower part. Fields relevant in both countries are in the middle rows in the table. Clearly, socio-economic policy is the most generally salient field, and the table shows also that budgetary politics was more directly important in government formation in the Netherlands. The variation between the cases with respect to the scope of negotiations on controversial issues (and thus the scope of the relevant part of the coalition agreement) appears also in table 10.1. The parties forming the Tindemans V coalition dealt with conflicts in only three policy fields, whereas the scope of negotiations over the coalition agreement of the Lubbers I government and the Kok I government included six policy fields. The Tindemans V coalition included more parties (five) than the two Dutch coalitions (two and three parties respectively). The scope of policy bargaining thus seems to decrease rather than increase with the number of parties in the coalition.

The overall picture of policy fields where coalition disputes emerged in government formation corresponds with the main subjects of government conflicts in Belgium in the Netherlands reported by Nousiainen (1993) in a study of internal processes within European cabinets. In Belgium, cabinet conflicts in the 1970s and 1980s were mostly on what were called 'cultural problems' (a broader category including language policy, regionalization and education policy), on budgetary and economic policy and on issues relating to justice and general administration (for which no clear equivalents can be found in the case studies, probably because these matters were departmental conflicts and not the type of interparty conflicts central in this book). The conflicts recorded for Dutch cabinets concern mainly the budget and economic policy, social affairs, and foreign affairs/defence and justice (Nousiainen, 1993). The issues of morality policy analyzed in the case studies in this book are within the jurisdictions of justice and social affairs distinguished by Nousiainen.

Types of Arrangements in Coalition Agreements

Table 10.2 summarizes the types of arrangements made in the five coalitions. The general pattern emerging here is that explicit compromises were most frequent. The most common way in which parties tried to resolve policy disputes during government formation was thus by writing down clear substantive commitments - this happened in 52 percent of the number of policy conflicts). These commitments entailed gains and concessions for all parties, and a balance was established often by linking issues for which the government formation arena provides opportunities. Both procedural and substantive implicit compromises are political formulas used to conceal or appease conflict, and these two types together occurred slightly less often, in 48 percent of the number of policy conflicts during government formation. Procedures however were much more rare (11 percent) than general intentions (37 percent). Matters on which the parties could not remove disagreement during government formation thus mostly were left vague. Only in a relatively small number of conflicts, parties were able to arrange how they would deal with the issue during the term in office of the government. The field in which this type of deal was most common was nuclear power, an issue involving value conflict and uncertainty.

Though the general picture is that explicit compromises were most frequent, this was not the case in all coalitions. In fact, as table 10.2 indicates, drawing up explicit compromises was more common in Belgium than in the Netherlands. As can be seen in table 10.1., this was done extensively in the field of regionalization – the domain in which large coalitions were made with the intention to carry through constitutional revisions. The two coalitions in which these explicit intentions onregionalization were made contained five parties with widely divergent viewpoints on the central issues (the most salient dimension in coalition formation was also the most controversial one), and the coalition agreement was used to

Table 10.1   Types of arrangements in policy fields (absolute figures)

Policy Field	Type of arrangement				where?*
	explicit	procedural	implicit	all	
language	2	–	–	2	Leburton
regionalization	18	3	1	22	Tindemans, Leburton
morality	1	–	3	4	Leburton, Lubbers
socio-economic	15	–	14	29	all
education	4	2	5	11	Leburton, Lubbers, Van Agt, Kok
budget	10	–	7	17	Lubbers, Van Agt, Kok, Tindemans
nuclear power	–	4	1	5	Van Agt, Lubbers
media	1	–	2	3	Lubbers
infrastructure	–	1	1	2	Kok
institutional reform	–	–	2	2	Kok
environment	–	1	–	1	Kok
	51	11	36	98	

* The number of times a coalition is mentioned in this column is the coalition's policy scope.

bridge the differences *ex ante* as much as possible. The same logic applies to the Kok I government, which was the one Dutch coalition with many explicit compromises. Most of these compromises were on socio-economic policy, and this was the field in which the coalition members PvdA (Social Democrats) and VVD (Liberals) stood farthest apart. In this coalition too, making explicit compromises was an investment on which the returns were expected during government life.

Tables 10.1 and 10.2 show that the broad scope of negotiations in the two most recent coalitions in the Netherlands does not go with detailed arrangements on all these matters. In the fields of nuclear power, the media, morality policy, institutional reform and infrastructure, deals were mostly implicit. Here, particularly the smaller parties used the coalition agreement for setting the agenda. But also on socio-economic and budgetary policy, implicit compromises were produced. The parties in the Lubbers I coalition did not hammer out detailed arrangements on all issues of socio-economic policy, and this is even more true for the Van Agt II government that preceded it. The Van Agt II coalition had a limited scope of policy bargaining, but as the case study in chapter 7 has shown, the nature of conflicts was constant sum or even zero sum (gains for one party were the losses for another), and this made it impossible for the parties to make explicit deals. During government formation, the choice seemed to be: no explicit deals, or no coalition.

Peace and Policy Effects of Political Deals

The observed patterns of conflict resolution during government formation in five coalitions illustrate that policy design under conditions of political conflict, mistrust and uncertainty involves two strategies: one is to make commitments that are as detailed and binding as possible, the other is to forgo clear commitments and keep options open. Both strategies were used, with different emphasis in the five coalitions.

Table 10.2   Types of arrangements in coalition agreements (percentages)

	Type of arrangement			
	explicit	procedural	implicit	
Coalition				
Leburton	58	17	25	(n=24)
Tindemans V	80	0	20	(n=15)
Van Agt II	33	20	47	(n=15)
Lubbers I	36	9	55	(n=22)
Kok I	55	9	36	(n=22)
average	52	11	37	(n=98)

What were the effects of these strategies? The costs of making explicit compromises may be high, but this may lead to lower costs of implementation. Costs are the efforts and time involved in formulating policy options and settling dispute. Conversely, substantive implicit compromises may be easier to reach, but more difficult to implement because the conflict is not really resolved. Procedural arrangements are distinct, in that they pertain directly to conflict management. The implicit element is that they are silent about policy contents, and the explicit element is that they specify how the coalition should handle the issue. The costs of making and implementing procedural arrangements both may be low, but the nondecisions about the issue may have their own costs.

For these reasons, one hypothesis was that explicit compromises are implemented without conflict. Substantive implicit compromises were expected to lead to new conflict, and lead to substantive decisions (the definition of implementation) less often than explicit compromises. The hypothesis on procedural implicit compromises was that they are implemented without conflict, the substantive effect of which is a nondecision.

The effects of the three types of arrangements are given in tables 10.3, 10.4 and 10.5. Effects in different policy fields are presented in table 10.6. Note that the first two types of effect in the tables (conflict prevented and compromise implemented) are not mutually exclusive, and that percentages do not add up to 100. The averages for all types of compromises (n=98), mentioned in table 10.6, are: 39 percent conflict prevented, 53 percent implementation, and 24 percent implementation without conflict.

Explicit Compromises and Policy Streamlining

A look at table 10.3 shows that the time and energy devoted to making explicit compromises in government formation has not led to an implementation process without costs. On average, 29 percent of the compromises was really implemented without conflict. The majority of explicit compromises even was not implemented at all, at least not in the form agreed during government formation. Parties either deviated from the agreement or they aborted implementation. This happened most dramatically in the governments that ended prematurely. Conflict remained absent in just over half the number of cases (51 percent), and this meant that the parties did not get into new trouble when implementing the deal, or that the matter was shelved because the government ended. This last result occurred particularly in the two Belgian coalitions and the Van Agt II coalition. The coalition agreement of the Tindemans V government had a large proportion of explicit compromises, made mostly on regionalization policy, and the early collapse of the five party government over this issue (explicit compromises) implied a very low performance in implementation. This applies also to the Van Agt II government, which foundered over socio-economic policy. For these governments, the percentages of conflict prevented conceal that the conflicts that did arise were lasting and fatal.

Much more positive were the effects during the Kok I government, which even managed to implement the majority of explicit compromises in the coalition agreement without new conflict. Compared to the other coalitions, the rate of implementation is also striking. The Lubbers I coalition had to deal with recurring

Table 10.3   Effects of explicit compromises (percentages)

	Effect			
	conflict prevented	implemented	implemented without conflict	
Coalition				
Leburton	43	50	29	(n=14)
Tindemans V	50	8	8	(n=12)
Van Agt II	60	20	20	(n=5)
Lubbers I	38	63	25	(n=8)
Kok I	67	83	58	(n=12)
average	51	47	29	(n=51)

Table 10.4   Effects of procedural implicit compromises (percentages)

	Effect			
	conflict prevented	implemented	implemented without conflict	
Coalition				
Leburton	50	75	50	(n=4)
Tindemans V	–	–	–	(n=0)
Van Agt II	100	67	67	(n=3)
Lubbers I	50	100	50	(n=2)
Kok I	0	100	0	(n=2)
average	55	82	45	(n=11)

Table 10.5   Effects of substantive implicit compromises (percentages)

	Effect			
	conflict prevented	implemented	implemented without conflict	
Coalition				
Leburton	0	33	0	(n=6)
Tindemans V	0	100	0	(n=3)
Van Agt II	29	0	0	(n=7)
Lubbers I	8	58	8	(n=12)
Kok I	38	88	38	(n=8)
average	17	53	11	(n=36)

Table 10.6   Effects of coalition agreements in different policy fields (percentages)

Policy Field	conflict prevented	implementation	Effect implementation without conflict	most common compromise	
language	100	100	100	Explicit	(n=2)
regionalization	41	9	9	Explicit	(n=22)
morality	25	25	25	Implicit	(n=4)
socio-economic	48	76	41	Explicit	(n=29)
education	27	64	9	Implicit	(n=11)
budget	35	59	24	Explicit	(n=17)
nuclear power	60	80	40	Procedural	(n=5)
media	0	0	0	Implicit	(n=3)
infrastructure	0	100	0	Implicit	(n=2)
institutional reform	0	50	0	Implicit	(n=2)
environment	0	100	0	Procedural	(n=1)
average	39	53	24		(n=98)

conflict much more often, but never the less also implemented nearly two thirds of the deals in the coalition agreement. The long duration of these coalitions is less an obvious reason for this than it may seem, as many things can happen to deals made at the beginning of such a long term in office. As parliamentary elections come closer, parties also have stronger electoral incentives to profile themselves rather than cooperate in enforcing deals made long ago. This is particularly true for socio-economic and budgetary policy, the fields in which the two most successful coalitions made most explicit compromises. The Leburton government was in office much shorter, but also this coalition implemented half the number of explicit compromises, which settled language dispute and education policy.

Though in absolute terms there is limited evidence for the hypothesis that explicit compromises streamline coalition policy making, it is thus important to appreciate that even explicit compromises in coalition agreements are always incomplete and involve uncertainty. The political and broader environment in which agreements need to be enforced is dynamic. Taking this into account, it is actually quite an achievement that parties making commitments without any legal basis or external enforcing authority also turn these early commitments into practice in almost half the number of cases, and without conflict in 29 percent of the cases.

Procedural Implicit Compromises and Risk Avoidance

The price for making procedural solutions is that no substantive policy decisions are made for some time, and this time horizon even may be beyond the end of the government. This is not a price for all, but given the existence of policy divergence, there is always at least one party that prefers a substantive change to the status quo. Procedures thus also entail concessions, and this makes enforcement not self evident. Did this type of arrangement have a freezing effect during the five government coalitions? Table 10.4 shows that this effect occurred in 82 percent of the cases, but it shows also that the heat of political dispute was not taken away in half the number of cases. 45 percent of the procedures were implemented without conflict. Since the primary function of this type of arrangement is to prevent conflict, this is a limited success. Ironically, the generally successful Kok I government had most difficulties with procedures, and for the troubled Van Agt II government the procedures on nuclear power were a blessing – for what this was worth. In conclusion, procedural implicit compromises mostly freeze policy making, but the desired peace mostly needs renegotiation.

Substantive Implicit Compromises and Boomeranging Conflict

Given the effects of explicit compromises and procedural arrangements, the effects of substantive implicit compromises shown in table 10.5 are mostly in the hypothesized direction. That is, the type of compromise in which intentions are general or vague leads to conflict much more often than the other types. Implementation without conflict is even quite rare (11 percent). In both Belgian coalitions, all implicit compromises gave rise to conflict. The successful Kok I government was least troubled by recurring conflict over implicit compromises, but this happened still in the majority of cases.

A less expected general finding however is that, on average, implicit compromises were implemented more often than explicit compromises (53 against 47 percent). A closer look at tables 10.3 and 10.5 shows that this difference can be attributed to the strongly varying effects during the Tindemans V government, in which only 8 percent (1) of the (12) explicit compromises and 100 percent of the (3) substantive implicit compromises was implemented. None the less, implementation was more successful than expected. Given that commitments were general and sometimes vague, the leeway for parties in implementation was much larger than in the case of explicit compromises. This increased the frequency of implementation – it was simply impossible to determine whether the parties deviated from the coalition agreement in the policy decisions they made. The costs of arriving at these decisions however were high; very few were implemented without conflict. Failure of implementation often was due to conflict, which occurred frequently in the parliamentary arena. The Leburton government and the Van Agt II government even collapsed after conflict over deals that were left vague.

Discount Rates and Political Costs of Deals

Parties involved in negotiations on a coalition agreement may use high discount rates, minimize costs and thus make cheap deals. But the patterns found in the effects of different arrangements suggest that such lower costs of making deals on coalition policy often lead to higher political costs of implementation. This conforms to the central theoretical proposition in transaction costs economics (Williamson, 1985). This perspective is useful for analyzing coalition agreements between political parties (Timmermans, 1999). Conflict occurred far more often when parties made substantive but general or vague implicit compromises during government formation than when they negotiated explicit compromises containing clear commitments (83 percent against 49 percent). Procedures containing postponements appeared to be, in relative terms, the best mechanism of political risk avoidance (45 percent was implemented without conflict), but this type of arrangement implies that no substantive decisions are taken for some fixed period. Whenever coalition peace was the most important shared goal, parties took a long term horizon (up to the normal length of the term in office) and procrastinated decisions. The proportion of this type of arrangements in the coalition agreements however was small.

Explicit compromises may be seen as investments on which the returns become visible during coalition life, but detailed deals on policy are also vulnerable. In a world that is changing constantly, fixed intentions that are declared sacrosanct may become obstacles. For this reason, it is not so surprising that explicit compromises were implemented less often than the other types of compromises. That is, the coalition parties within the government or in parliament (seldom allowing much influence for external parties) made modifications in the explicit compromises to the extent they could agree on this, or dropped the plans and moved to an alternative to the agreement. One government, Tindemans V, broke down when centrifugal forces in implementing the plans on regionalization went beyond control. None the less, almost half of the explicit compromises (47 percent) *were* implemented in their original form, and 29 percent was implemented without generating new conflict.

Implicit compromises were more often implemented, but as said this is also because they allowed much more discretion to the coalition parties. If the coalition agreement said that the government would 'reconsider the priorities for next year' or 'propose legislation on abortion', the real political work was still ahead. Nearly always this work involved extensive coalition conflict management. Cheap deals thus often had expensive consequences.

Success and Failure in Different Policy Fields

The effects of arrangements in the different policy fields are shown in table 10.6. No distinction between types of arrangements is made, only the most common type of compromise in each policy field is mentioned in table 10.6. In all fields except language, regionalization, morality policy and media policy, arrangements were more often implemented than that they prevented conflict. This means that despite the investments made by parties during government formation (and which varied between the types of deals), implementation still involved considerable costs. The 'conflict prevention' effect of deals on regionalization should be attributed in part to the early breakdown of the Tindemans V coalition in 1978, which precluded that a number of compromises on this matter were dealt with. For a similar reason, the premature end of the Van Agt II government in 1982 explains part of the conflict prevention effect of deals on education and budgetary policy.

There is clear variation between policy fields in terms of overall success and failure. In some fields, things mostly went wrong, and in other fields compromises worked well. Effects in the fields of language policy and media policy are most straightforward: the explicit deals on language streamlined policy making, and on media issues the implicit compromises in the coalition agreement were completely dysfunctional. Also relatively successful were the compromises on socio-economic issues, on budgetary policy, and the procedural arrangements on nuclear (defence) power. Fields in which failure was predominant were regionalization, institutional reform, and morality policy. The procedural arrangement on environmental policy in the Kok I coalition was implemented, but did not prevent conflict. Effects were mixed in the fields of education and infrastructure, where deals often were implemented but this involved controversy.

Are the effects in policy fields also related to the most common type of compromise in each of these fields? This does not seem to be true for implementation as one effect. The average percentage of implemented arrangements (all types) was 53. Though in three of the four fields that lacked substantive success (less than 50 percent implementation), implicit compromises were most frequent, no clear pattern emerges in the seven policy fields where a higher percentage of implementation was reached (between 59 and 100 percent). In three fields, explicit compromises were most common, in two fields procedural arrangements dominated, and in two fields, substantive implicit compromises were used most). These findings suggest that for implementation as an effect of coalition agreements, the policy field makes more difference than the type of deal.

The type of arrangement seems to have been more relevant to prevention of conflict in the different fields. Given the average of 39 percent conflict prevention (all types of arrangements), there were four fields in which deals had a more peaceful effect (41 to 100 percent conflict prevented). In three of these fields, explicit compromises prevailed, and in one field the most common type of arrangement was procedural. In five of the seven fields where conflict prevention was less successful (from 35 percent to 0 percent conflict prevented), substantive implicit compromises were the most common type of deal (and in the field where explicit compromises were most common, budgetary policy, the percentage for conflict prevention was still 35). A similar pattern emerges when considering the arrangements that were implemented without conflict. In four of the five fields where this effect occurred in at least 24 percent of the cases (the average), the most common deal was the explicit compromise or (in one field) the procedure. And in four of the six fields where conflictless implementation was rare (9 percent or less), the deal was a general implicit compromise.

These general findings sustain the idea that conflict is an important type of costs throughout coalition life, and that by choosing a strategy of making explicit deals in government formation, coalition parties reduce the costs of policy making during the life of the government.

Loci of Failure

Implementation and prevented conflict are effects of deals that indicate the functions of coalition agreements. The performance of these functions is a result of interactions within multiple arenas, formal and informal, and for conflict prevention this is evident. But policy decisions as substantive effects of deals are taken in the government and in parliament. In the case studies in this book, formal parliamentary approval or ratification has been used as a condition for implementation of deals containing substantive intentions. Procedural arrangements were considered to be implemented if ministers and parliamentary groups observed the specifications given in the procedures. There may be many other effects, direct and indirect, and immediate and long term, but only authoritative decisions taken in the constitutional bodies of parliamentary democracy were considered to be implementation. Implementation thus is understood as political implementation of political deals.

This perspective is important also for analyzing failure. If implementation was considered successful when a formal decision with the same content as the political deal was taken during the term of the government, failure is the stagnation of this process. This has occurred in many different arenas. Cabinet ministers sometimes simply lost faith in the coalition agreement, and parliamentary parties have sought ways to escape commitments that were expected to bring them electoral misfortune. Even party branches outside the constitutional policy making bodies have been sites where the political deals from the coalition agreements were unscrambled. Informal arenas of coalition governance were used for steering implementation of deals and for managing coalition conflict, but *because* these were the most important sites of high politics, the likelihood of failure also increased compared to arenas where only routine matters were dealt with.

Table 10.7 summarizes the loci of failure in the different policy fields. A mixed locus consists of ministers and parliamentary leaders. Compromises on language, infrastructure, environmental policy and nuclear power were all or nearly all implemented, and are excluded from the table. In Belgium, deals on regionalization policy were least successful, and failure in this field occurred in both an extraparliamentary arena (the informal committee, or 'junta', of party presidents) and in the public arena of parliament. This was the arena where prime minister Tindemans, challenged by the parliamentary parties and even by part of his own group, decided to give up coalition cooperation in 1978. The coalition crisis in 1974 on state intervention in industry however resulted from internal deadlock within the Leburton cabinet.

In the Netherlands, the breakdown in 1982 of the Van Agt II coalition over budgetary and socio-economic policy happened within the cabinet. Much less dramatic was the decision by the Kok I cabinet not to implement an implicit compromise on city provinces (institutional reform). Other cases of failure in the Dutch coalitions mostly occurred in arenas of mixed composition or in parliament. These were the loci of failure on media policy, morality issues and education. In these fields, substantive implicit compromises were most common, and the elaboration of these deals was costly and risky. It stagnated in the arena where exposure to the broader public was largest and the electoral consequences of policy decisions (even those following from the coalition agreement) were felt most.

Table 10.7   Loci of failure in policy fields

	Arena			
	cabinet	parliament	mixed	extra-parliamentary
Policy field				
regionalization		x		x
morality		x	x	
socio-economic	x			
education		x	x	
budget	x			
media		x		
institutional reform	x			

Coping with the Problem of Enforcement

Arrangements in coalition agreements are not legally binding nor self policing. Monitoring implementation of a policy deal may be easier if this deal contains clear cut intentions, and thus if parties have invested in doing this. It may be that such investments, as sunk costs, induce parties to remain loyal because they realize the trouble of renegotiation. But in the real world of coalition politics the schemes of costs and benefits may change rapidly for individual parties. This is why enforcement of coalition agreements is more complex than monitoring a single deal: the benefits of cooperation in implementing a deal containing major concessions often depend on implementation of *other* deals. A coalition partner may need payoffs from other policies to remain faithful. If this is not possible, the specificity of the deal even may be counterproductive, because the losses are so visible. In such situations, the problem of enforcement becomes really serious.

Coalition governance however does not take place in a Hobbesian state of nature. Parties care about their reputation, and norms and structures for coalition governance have emerged. The principle of *pacta sunt servanda* (agreements must be observed) is such a norm, and a complement to this norm is the mechanism of reciprocal control. Parties cooperate because defection can lead to retaliation by others, or even to use of the 'big gun': the threat to bring down the government.

The mechanism of reciprocal control may seem an invisible hand, but it requires busy interparty traffic. For this, structural conditions may be relevant, such as the size of the coalition, the internal unity within the participant parties, and the presence of informal arenas of conflict management. Another structural coalition property that may facilitate enforcement of agreements is the extent to which negotiators in government formation have taken a cabinet seat. Prime ministerial role performance is also relevant, as this is the office of coalition coordination. Personal relationships among cabinet ministers may influence the willingness to cooperate. Finally, developments in the economic environment may allow budget expansion or confront parties with the need to set priorities and make hard choices. The less these developments were anticipated during government formation, the more likely it is that economic indicators are used as ammunition by parties contesting enforcement of the coalition agreement.

These different conditions for enforcement were considered in the case studies, and their impact varied. The least tangible factor was personal relationships, which seems to have played a part mainly within the sphere of the cabinet. When ministers did not like each other, as in the case of prime minister Dries van Agt (Christian Democrats, CDA) and vice prime Joop den Uyl (Social Democrats, PvdA) between 1981 and 1982, this reduced the willingness to cooperate when the political stakes were high. But the personal factor did not cause failure, and it seems to have been a residual factor in the other coalitions. The structural conditions for enforcement seem to have been more generally relevant for explaining effects. The way in which these factors facilitated implementation of the coalition agreement are examined below.

A Multiplicity of Coalition Governance Arenas

One assumption was that the difficulty of enforcing coalition agreements increases as the arenas in which deals are implemented become more different from the government formation arena, where the deals were made. In government formation, party spokespersons negotiate in an informal setting, with few formal rules constraining policy formulation. The time for building a new government is limited, but the setting allows parties to engage in parallel processing: issues can be linked and dealt with simultaneously. When it comes to making concessions, negotiators are delegates of parties realizing that internal unity must be preserved, to avoid that their bargaining power is undermined.

If the enforcement of compromises on coalition policy were to take place only in the formal arenas of the collective cabinet and parliament, inefficiency and the risk of stagnation would be high. This is the reason why informal arenas of coalition governance have emerged, and why enforcement of the coalition agreement often was transferred to such arenas before formal policy decisions were taken. In the arenas of coalition governance, attempts were made to confirm commitments made earlier, or to settle disputes over these commitments.

The types and properties of informal arenas have varied between coalitions and between countries. As consensus systems, Belgium and the Netherlands have multiple types of policy making arenas, but for matters of high politics, political arenas are particularly important (Timmermans, 2001). In the Netherlands, internal and informal cabinet arenas were important, as well as the 'turret consultations' taking place in the mixed arena composed of ministers and the parliamentary leaders of the coalition parties. Since the early 1980s, this last arena is the site where the most serious conflicts are managed (Andeweg and Timmermans, forthcoming). Most decisions carrying implementation of deals on budgetary and socio-economic policy based on the coalition agreement were prepared in the 'pentagon' (Van Agt II, Lubbers I) and the 'hexagon' (Kok I), the group of first responsible ministers in these fields. The Dutch governmental decisions in the early 1980s on nuclear weapons were prepared within an informal committee of ministers created *ad hoc*. In the Van Agt II case, the pentagon really was a centre of political warfare in which centrifugal forces were hard to contain. The coalition crisis in May 1982 however occurred in the collective cabinet arena when a formal vote was held on a proposal fleshing out an implicit compromise from the coalition agreement. In the Lubbers I coalition, the turret meetings in the mixed arena were crucial for conflict containment in all fields, but they could not prevent that deals on education, morality issues and media policy largely were unimplemented. During the Kok I coalition, this mixed arena produced more generally positive peace and policy effects, which were ratified in the cabinet and in parliament.

In Belgium, arenas within the government were less central in the process of enforcement, and seem to have been most important in the fields of budgetary and socio-economic policy. The typical site for management of the most dangerous conflicts in Belgium is the arena external of the cabinet (Andeweg and Timmermans, forthcoming), and external arenas were also the most important for enforcement of the coalition agreement. Broad parliamentary committees were formed for regionalization and education policy, but conflict containment did not always imply implementation of deals. During the Leburton government, the special committee on regionalization even was unable to turn the deals into legislation, and implementation was transferred to the cabinet. In the cabinet however deadlock occurred over state intervention in industry. During the Tindemans V coalition, the most conspicuous coalition committee was the group of party presidents. This committee had been prominent in drafting legislation on regionalization, following the special coalition pacts made at Egmont and Stuyvenberg, but eventually the project foundered in the parliamentary arena.

Thus, informal coalition governance arenas have been used extensively for conflict containment and implementing deals, but they were not always effective. For one thing, the locus of high politics shifted to formal arenas at critical stages of conflict, and the result was coalition collapse in the cases of Leburton (cabinet), Tindemans V (parliament) and Van Agt II (cabinet). In the 'invisible' trajectory of implementation, the coalition machinery produced the most substantive results in the fields of budgetary and socio-economic policy, and was less functional in fields of 'immaterial' policy. In these fields, the parliamentary arena was more important, and there maintaining coalition discipline and internal party discipline were more difficult.

Voice or Loyalty within Coalition Parties

The unitary actor assumption has long been upheld in coalition theory, but for coalition life it is not realistic. None the less, maintaining a level of internal party loyalty and discipline are important in the process of implementing coalition agreements. Divisions and party revolts beyond control of the leadership – provided that the party leadership itself is not divided – weaken the centralization of authority in government coalitions (Strøm and Müller, 2001). Internally divided parties may be more vulnerable to attempts by external parties to form legislative coalitions, which may be directly or indirectly 'prohibited' by the coalition agreement.

The case studies indicate that the degree of internal party unity makes a difference to enforcement of coalition agreements. In Belgium, the traditional parties were divided internally over *la question communautaire*, and in both coalitions, the prominents least supportive of the plans in this field took a cabinet seat. Moreover, in the Tindemans V coalition, divisions within the Flemish Christian Democratic party (CVP) were reinforced by rivalry for the party leadership. The institutionalized factions within the CVP did not lead to trouble in the field of socio-economic policy.

In the Netherlands, internal party divisions seem to have been controlled relatively well within internal cabinet arenas, but less in parliament. Cabinet decisions on nuclear weapons for example obtained a parliamentary majority only with the support of opposition parties. Elaboration of the mostly general implicit compromises on immaterial issues in the Lubbers I coalition agreement foundered in part because the parliamentary groups did not feel like rubber stamping policies developed by the cabinet. On these matters, no substantive agreement had been reached between the parliamentary groups of the CDA and the VVD during government formation, and in a coalition that was already extremely tight in the fields of budgetary and socio-economic policy, the parties held on to their principles and deferred decisions to the next government. With different parties and with more generally positive effects, the Kok I coalition shows a similar pattern. In the Dutch coalitions, the lack of internal party discipline in enforcing a number of deals thus was due to 'divisions' relating to the constitutional separation of powers: the coalition parties in parliament emphasized their independence from the cabinet ministers. This position is a fundamental challenge of the practice of coalition agreements, but it was an exception, not the rule.

Coalition Founding Fathers as Exegetes

The enforcement capacity of coalition governance arenas depends not only on the informal setting and on internal party cohesion, but also on the presence of negotiators. Negotiators of deals in government formation may be promoted to the office of cabinet minister or they continue their career in parliament. Thus in this respect coalition governance arenas may resemble the government formation arena to varying degrees. Presence of the 'founding fathers' in important arenas, particularly those internal to the cabinet, is assumed to be conducive to the implementation of deals. In this way, commitments are internalized in the policy making arenas. For deals that are vague or ambiguous, former negotiators are the most qualified exegetes because they may be able to read between the lines. Outsiders are assumed to be less inclined to implement arrangements because they may feel confronted with *faits accomplis* that infringe in their ministerial autonomy.

The case studies contain empirical evidence for this assumption, but with the Van Agt II government as a notable exception. In this government, participation in the cabinet of two antagonistic party leaders that had made vague deals with incompatible intentions did not bring much enlightenment. The trouble in this coalition was also that where informal arenas were needed most, they were used least. This was because fundamental mistrust among the Christian Democrats (CDA) and Social Democrats (PvdA) pushed decision making to the collective level, the formal cabinet arena.

In the other coalitions, the participation or nonparticipation of negotiators in the government mostly relates to the degree of success in implementing deals. In the Belgian governments, few negotiators on regionalization were present, and failure was the main result in this field (in following governments formations, this lesson was drawn [De Ridder, 1989]). Negotiators on education policy deals took a seat in the Leburton government, and the deals were implemented. The Lubbers I and Kok I governments show a similar pattern. The fields in which success in implementing compromises was large (budgetary and socio-economic policy) were the ministerial jurisdiction of former negotiators. Where success was limited or absent, cabinet ministers had been less involved in government formation. It should be noted however that in the fields of media policy, education and morality issues, the locus of failure (table 10.7) was not an internal cabinet arena but a parliamentary arena. In this arena the control possibilities for party spokespersons in government formation are more limited, because in many other respects the arena differs widely from the government formation arena. In parliament, enforcement of coalition deals is weakened by incentives to emphasize differences in party profiles.

Prime Ministers as Coalition Coordinators

The key role of prime ministers is to preserve the harmony within the coalition, and this includes guidance in implementing policy deals and arbitration in conflicts. But not all prime ministers are able to take distance from their own party interests. Clearly, the chances of successful enforcement of coalition agreements increase if the first role perception is dominant. Prime ministers actively taking sites in struggles of interpretation may win, but in countries (such as Belgium and the Netherlands) where the competencies vested in this office are rather limited, this strategy is not likely to lead to long term success, at least not for the coalition.

The two prime ministers that were most explicit in their policy position were Leo Tindemans and Dries van Agt. Both prime ministers felt only lukewarm support – if any support at all – for the coalition agreement. In fact, Tindemans had not been his party's most prominent negotiator, and Van Agt even had withdrawn as his party's first spokesman during government formation. The point of lacking support applies also, if somewhat less, to Edmund Leburton, who as a French speaker had difficulty establishing authority as the head of a bilingual government. From a coalition perspective, their governments failed, and the prime ministerial strategy seems to have contributed to this.

The coordinating role was played more effectively by Ruud Lubbers and Wim Kok. Particularly in the fields of budgetary and socio-economic policy, the prime ministerial part in enforcing the coalition agreement seems to have made a difference. In the case of Lubbers, however, the discretion left in compromises (implicit, but sometimes also explicit) was used often to propose alternatives if conflict over a deal formed an obstacle to make substantive decisions. As a Christian Democrat, this prime minister had mixed feelings about some of the deals on immaterial policy (euthanasia, equal treatment, media), but failure on these matters occurred in parliament, where the span of prime ministerial control is more limited than in the cabinet. Prime minister Kok appeared to be focused strongly on coalition discipline in implementation of the coalition agreement, even when this led to tensions within his own party, the PvdA.

Policy Payoffs, Agenda Management, and Cooperation

Structural properties of coalitions are relevant conditions for enforcement of agreements, but the setting of coalition governance alone does not produce reciprocal control. The other key question therefore is how the coalition keeps the process of implementation going. Again, the enforcement problem arises because compromises made in packages can become more difficult to accept when dealt with separately. Loyalty and the limit of tolerance for parties in policy making include a time element, and parties may become opportunistic.

The assumption was that coalition size is related inversely to the possibilities of reciprocal control among parties. Though the number of cases for assessment of this particular assumption is limited, the empirical effects of the agreements in five coalitions do not contain much evidence. The least successful and the most successful coalitions (Van Agt II and Kok I) both contained three parties. The strength of reciprocal control did vary between the coalitions, but the dynamics of this enforcement mechanism must be influenced by something else. For example, the patterns of findings show that coalitions with a broad policy scope in the coalition agreement (Lubbers I, Kok I) have higher implementation rates than coalitions that negotiated deals in only a few policy fields (Tindemans V, Van Agt II). At first sight this may be surprising, because in this analysis, a broader scope means that more different issues were controversial during coalition formation. Apparently, the parties anticipated where the trouble for the coalition would be and invested in making deals in these fields. The broad range of deals provided more possibilities for balancing payoffs for parties over time.

This last possibility relates to a more general point: parties invest in a coalition because they expect policy payoffs. For institutional reasons, cabinets and parliaments cannot consider many different subjects at the same time; the capacity of cabinets and parliaments for parallel processing is limited. But serial processing of matters of high politics may make coalition parties impatient. Single deals often contain less balanced payoffs than broader packages of deals. They may even contain major concessions that one party was willing to make because it was compensated on another issue. The risk of opportunism is related to the perception of individual parties about such compensations. If no other policy payoffs are within sight, the discount rate for a party goes down, and this may destabilize the coalition. Electoral prospects may then be included in the strategic calculations. Thus, for a stable allocation of payoffs among coalition parties, agenda management is crucial, and this requires a degree of hierarchy (Timmermans, 1994: 117–119).

To what extent have the coalitions been able to manage their policy agendas, what Riker (1986) called a form of 'heresthetics'? As noted, the scope of the agenda incorporated into the coalition agreement is likely to make a difference, although parties can introduce other issues not considered in government formation. New issues may be really important or be used to create sidepayments.

The case studies suggest three types of process. Two end up in deadlock, one is the route of coalition success. First, the worst case scenario is that enforcement does not even begin, because the coalition agreement contains barely any issue diversity and directs the attention of parties to policies on which they did not really reach substantive agreement. This was the situation in the Van Agt II coalition, where the agenda had a narrow scope and contained incompatible intentions. The policies preferred most by one party were the most resisted by the other. Hardly any possibilities for agenda management existed, and the constant messages of economic bad news further narrowed down the set of alternatives. This resulted in early collapse, and the coalition agreement, compared to a 'plate of spaghetti' because of the many loose ends and chaos at the coalition dinner table, was a negative example for the following government (Lubbers I).

The second type of process is one of decline in enforcement. Here, reciprocal control is affected by the cumulative experiences of parties over time. Agenda management at central level, if attempted at all, is not done in the collective interest of the coalition. It is more a form of what Lax and Sebenius (1991) call 'strategic sequencing'. During the Leburton coalition, the Christian Democrats benefited from the relatively quick implementation of the compromises on school policy, on which the other parties had made concessions. The Socialists however were awaiting implementation of intentions on socio-economic policy, about which particularly the Liberals were not too enthusiast. The Socialists, still a unitary party with its strongest electoral basis in Wallonia, wanted financial injections for the troubled heavy industry in that area. Much attention in the coalition however was centred on regionalization, which took a large part of the cabinet agenda after school policy was settled. For the Socialists, the tolerance limit was reached after one year in office, and the party withdrew from the government. Negative prospects of policy payoffs in the future also were a reason for collapse of the Tindemans V coalition, but in this case the decision to give up cooperation was taken by the party that had benefited most. The CVP made gains in the field of socio-economic policy, which was the first part of the coalition agreement. The more ambitious part however was on regionalization, and on this matter the perception of an influential group within the CVP, including the prime minister was that the French speaking part of the country would benefit at the costs of the Dutch speaking part. The Socialists however were pressing for progress in this field, not least because they had electoral interests in policies favouring the French speaking voters. In this coalition too, the agenda was limited in scope, and this meant that the deals on regionalization, mostly specific and thus with visible concessions, became the subject of direct confrontation. Prime minister Tindemans did not want to receive the blame for a policy 'selling out' the Dutch speaking Flanders, and gave up coalition cooperation. Thus, in these cases, failing agenda management and opportunism (all relating to deals in the coalition agreement) led to the early end of the coalition.

The cases of the Lubbers I and the Kok I coalition show the third type of process, in which reciprocal control works relatively well. These two positive cases also were coalitions in which the prime minister had been involved directly in writing the agreement and, in office, managed the coalition agenda without taking sides. They differed in economic circumstances, which were becoming more positive during the Kok I government. Despite conflict, which demonstrates that faith is not blind and opportunism never absent, many of the deals were processed in such a way that all coalition parties obtained policy payoffs over time. The conflict in the Kok I coalition between D66 and the VVD over the deal on the referendum (payoff for D66), the 'need of compensations' (VVD) and the subsequent mitigation (VVD: 'it is not our preference, but we are loyal because we see the compensations in the coalition agreement') illustrates that reciprocal control is visible also in political language. During the Lubbers I coalition in the 1980s, much of this language even was invented, as an expression of the tightness of the coalition agreement. Economic conditions may limit or enlarge the possibilities for keeping all coalition parties happy, and the findings on the Lubbers I and Kok I coalitions suggest that this was easier during the last of these two governments. But this factor carries weight in coalition politics through the constructions that parties make – how they define or redefine the problem and what new solutions they see. The effects of the Lubbers I coalition however show also that implementation mostly was uncompleted in the fields of immaterial policy. This qualifies what was said about enforcement, but it does not speak against the strength of reciprocal control. The reason is that also in these fields, the mostly implicit compromises were placed on the agenda and processed in relative balance with other matters, but delaying tactics in parliament prevented that legislation was adopted before the end of the term.

Enforcement of coalition agreements thus is a process in which agenda management is a key element because it limits or extends the possibilities for reciprocal control among coalition partners. But agenda management requires centralization, for which informal coalition governance arenas with properties similar to the government formation arena are helpful. This is suggested by the way in which the presence or absence of structural conditions for enforcement relates to effects of policy deals. Informal arenas in which the prime minister coordinates and arbitrates, where former negotiators are present and from where internal party discipline can be assured, contribute to implementation of coalition agreements. They thus reduce the costs of enforcement during the term in office. The findings in the case studies also suggest that investments in policy deals before the start of the coalition make a difference. Though opportunism is always a risk, explicit compromises and procedural arrangements prevent conflict and are implemented without conflict more often than implicit compromises.

Conclusion

The varying ways in which parties deal with controversial issues when forming a coalition government have different consequences for coalition life. Negotiated deals on controversial issues may not exhaust all possible sources of conflict, but they are an important point of departure for coalition governments in Belgium and the Netherlands. Controversial issues can be placed on the agenda and policy decisions even may be precooked, and the scope of action of the government coalition also can be limited by not placing issues on the agenda or by procrastinating substantive decisions. The rationale for parties doing this is that they see coalition agreements as a mechanism for conflict prevention and for increasing the efficiency of coalition policy making. Peterson et al. (1983: 74) have called policy formulation a cumulative process. The effects of coalition agreements indicate that this is true for coalition governments between their formation and end, and to an extent even policy cumulation from one coalition to the next has taken place. But this longer term element in the policy making process is more erratic, and it was not central in this book.

The coalition agreements of the Belgian and Dutch governments analyzed in this study were relevant, but not always in the ways envisioned by optimists during government formation. First, coalition agreements do have an agenda function – they formed a major part of the coalition agenda in each of the five cases. The agenda set in government formation contained issues on which substantive deals were made, but only half of all deals were explicit compromises containing clear commitments, prefabricated policy decisions. Most of the other deals were also substantive but implicit, containing general, vague or even ambiguous intentions. These were formulated to conceal persisting disagreement. The costs of making this type of deal may have been lower, but the gains also were much harder to accomplish, because conflict mostly boomeranged back into the coalition. With respect to this element of conflict, limitation of the scope of action of the government through procedural arrangements was found to be most effective. This way of handling issues however was not common, one obvious reason being that coalitions are supposed to *take* substantive policy decisions. Making explicit compromises involved higher transaction costs, but the costs of implementation, with substantive effects, were lower than for implicit compromises. This was particularly the case in the fields of budgetary and socio-economic policy, which in all five coalitions were very important for distributing policy payoffs among the coalition partners. The many deals on issues in these fields were implemented or modified, for which economic indicators were used. These indicators sometimes were used as ammunition in heated battles. In cases of deviation from the agreement, the deals still were points of reference, even in the Van Agt II coalition with its declining life expectancy. Also in other fields this happened, but with less substantive effects. For example, an 'editorial committee' of party prominents in the Tindemans V coalition set out to 'fill in the possible gaps' in the Egmont pact on regionalization, as it as was called somewhat euphemistically (KHA, 1977: 707). The efforts did not lead to policy decisions during the term of the government, but the renegotiated deals returned prominently onto the agenda of the next governments in the 1980s.

Making political deals in government formation is a process of weeks or perhaps several months, but enforcement of these deals takes years, and this requires a high discount rate. Parties need to be patient if implementation of single deals does not bring them the rewards they are waiting for. Reciprocal control is the mechanism that keeps parties from being opportunistic. It is an enforcement mechanism endogenous to the coalition – no external authority exists. Mutual control between parties also included commitments to refrain from building *ad hoc* legislative coalitions with parties outside the coalition. The mechanism of reciprocal control itself depends in part on management of the policy agenda, and the findings in this book show that variation in effects of coalition agreements can be explained in part by the way in which agenda management was organized, both through structures and through strategies of the central coalition leadership.

Both in Belgium and the Netherlands, the increased electoral volatility since the 1970s has reinforced the incentive for political parties to profile themselves, and to mistrust others. The bargaining system in which coalition governments in these two countries are made and maintained is multipolar and multidimensional – it contains sufficient variation in coalitionable parties and issues salient to these parties to make coalition bargaining complex and often protracted. The 1990s even have shown a further increase in competitiveness.

But this chronic situation is also the main reason why parties negotiate coalition agreements. It is an expression of the fundamental tension in coalition systems between standing apart and sitting together. Coalition agreements may reduce mistrust and uncertainty, and this motivates parties to invest in deals over controversial issues. Such investments may protect the coalition from falling apart. But the tension is not removed by negotiating deals for coalition agreements. Mechanisms for enforcing agreements are necessary to prevent opportunistic behaviour.

This book has explored the ways in which this enforcement is organized, what the conditions for success may be, and how types of deals in coalition agreements may make a difference. The empirical focus was on coalition governments in Belgium and the Netherlands, but the concepts and lines of argument need not be confined to these cases and countries. In recent comparative work (Müller and Strøm, 2000; Strøm, Müller and Bergman, forthcoming), the general features of coalition agreements and mechanisms of coalition governance in Western Europe have received systematic attention. In the history of coalition research since the 1960s, this attention is an important new development. The aim of this book is to bring the development in what we know about the things that coalition governments do a step further.

Bibliography

Andeweg, R.B. (1985), 'The Netherlands. Cabinet Committees in a Coalition Cabinet', in Mackie, Th.T. and Hogwood, B.W. (eds), *Unlocking the Cabinet. Cabinet Structures in Comparative Perspective*, Sage, London/Beverly Hills/ New Delhi, pp. 138–54.

Andeweg, R.B. (1989), 'The Politics of Less. A Description of Changes in Financial Decisionmaking in the Netherlands', paper presented at ECPR Joint Sessions of Workshops, Paris, 10–15 April 1989.

Andeweg, R.B. and Bakema, W. (1994), 'The Netherlands: Ministers and Cabinet Policy', in Laver, M. and Shepsle, K.A. (eds), *Cabinet Ministers and Parliamentary Government*, Cambridge University Press, New York, pp. 56–72.

Andeweg, R.B. and Timmermans, A. (forthcoming), 'Conflict Management in Coalition Government', in Strøm, K., Müller, W.C. and Bergman, T. (eds), *Coalition Governance in Parliamentary Democracies*, Oxford University Press, Oxford.

Axelrod, R.A. (1970), *Conflict of Interest. A Theory of Divergent Goals with Applications to Politics*, Markham, Chicago.

Baron, D.P. (1991), 'A Spatial Bargaining Theory of Government Formation in Parliamentary Systems', *American Political Science Review*, vol. 85, pp. 137–65.

Baron, D.P. (1993), 'Government Formation and Endogenous Parties', *American Political Science Review*, vol. 87, pp. 34–47.

Beleid Beschouwd (1981–98), Dutch newspaper.

Blondel, J. (1988), 'Cabinet Structures and Decision-Making Processes in Western Europe', *European Journal of Political Research*, vol. 16, pp. 115–23.

Blondel, J. and Cotta, M. (eds) (1996), *Party and Government*, Macmillan, London.

Blondel, J. and Müller-Rommel, F. (eds) (1993), *Governing Together. The Extent and Limits of Joint Decision-Making in Western European Cabinets*, Macmillan, London.

Bogdanor, V. (1983), *Coalition Government in Western Europe*, Heinemann, London.

Bovend'Eert, P.P.T. (1988), *Regeerakkoorden en Regeringsprograms. Een Wetenschappelijke Proeve op het Gebied van de Rechtsgeleerdheid*, Sdu, 's-Gravenhage.

Brassine, J. and Mabille, X. (1978), 'La Crise Politique d' Octobre 1978', *Courrier Hebdomadaire du Centre de Recherche et d' Information Sociale et Politique*, no. 817 and 819.

Browne, E.C. and Dreijmanis, J. (eds) (1982), *Government Coalitions in Western Democracies*, Longman, New York.

Browne, E. and Franklin, M. (1986), 'Editors' Introduction: New Directions in Coalition Research', *Legislative Studies Quarterly*, vol. 11, pp. 469–83.

Browne, E., Frendreis, J. and Gleiber, D. (1986), 'The Dissolution of Governments in Scandinavia: A Critical Events Perspective', *Scandinavian Political Studies*, vol. 9, pp. 93–110.

Budge, I. and Farlie, D. (1983), 'Party Competition – Selective Emphasis or Direct Confrontation? An Alternative View with Data', in Daalder, H. and Mair, P. (eds), *Western European Party Systems. Continuity and Change*, Sage, London/ Beverly Hills/New Delhi, pp. 267–305.

Budge, I. and Keman, H. (1990), *Parties and Democracy. Coalition Formation and Government Functioning in Twenty States*, Oxford University Press, Oxford.

Budge, I. and Laver, M. (1986), 'Office Seeking and Policy Pursuit in Coalition Theory', *Legislative Studies Quarterly*, vol. 11, pp. 485–506.

Budge, I., Robertson, D. and Hearl, D. (eds) (1987), *Ideology, Strategy and Party Change*, Cambridge University Press, Cambridge.

Covell, M. (1982), 'Agreeing to Disagree: Elite Bargaining and the Revision of the Belgian Constitution', *Canadian Journal of Political Science*, vol. 15, pp. 451–69.

De Ridder, H. (1982), *De Keien van de Wetstraat*, Davidsfonds, Leuven.

De Ridder, H. (1989), *Sire, Geef me Honderd Dagen*, Davidsfonds, Leuven.

De Ridder, M.M. and Fraga, L.R. (1986), 'The Brussels Issue in Belgian Politics', *West European Politics*, pp. 376–92.

De Standaard, Flemish newspaper.

De Swaan, A. (1973), *Coalition Theories and Cabinet Formation. A Study of Formal Theories of Coalition Formation Applied to Nine European Parliaments after 1918*, Elsevier, Amsterdam.

Dewinter, L., Timmermans, A. and Dumont, P. (2000), 'Belgium: On Government Agreements, Evangelists, Followers, and Heretics', in Müller, W.C. and Strøm, K. (eds), *Coalition Governments in Western Europe*, Oxford University Press, Oxford, pp. 300–55.

Dittrich, K.L.L.M., Cohen, J. and Rutgers, V. (1983), *Het Einde van een Tijdperk. Verslag van de Kabinetsformatie 1981 en 1982*, Rijksuniversiteit Limburg, Maastricht.

Dodd, L.C. (1976), *Coalitions in Parliamentary Government*, Princeton University Press, Princeton.

Gamson, W. (1961), 'A Theory of Coalition Formation', *American Sociological Review*, vol. 26, pp. 373–82.

Gilbert, M. (1993), 'Agreements, Coercion, and Obligation', *Ethics*, vol. 103, pp. 679–706.

Handelingen Tweede Kamer, Annals of the Second Chamber, the Netherlands.

Hardin, R. (1990), 'Trusting Persons, Trusting Institutions', in Zeckhauser, R.J. (ed) *Strategy and Choice*, Cambridge University Press, Cambridge, pp. 185–209.

Hobbes, T. (1651, edition 1968), *Leviathan*, edited and introduced by C.B. Macpherson, Penguin, Harmondsworth.

Kamer van Volksvertegenwoordigers (1973–78), Annals of the Chamber of Representatives, Belgium.

Keesings Historisch Archief (1973–98), Dutch edition of Keesings Contemporary Archives.

Klingemann, H.D., Hofferbert, R.I. and Budge, I. (eds) (1994), *Parties, Policies, and Democracy*, St. Martin's Press, New York.

Laver, M.J. and Budge, I. (eds) (1992), *Party Policy and Government Coalitions*, St. Martin's Press, New York.

Laver, M. and Hunt, W.B. (1992), *Policy and Party Competition*, Routledge, New York.

Laver, M. and Schofield, N. (1990), *Multiparty Government. The Politics of Coalition in Europe*, Oxford University Press, Oxford.

Laver, M. and Shepsle, K.A. (1990), 'Coalitions and Cabinet Government', *American Political Science Review*, vol. 84, pp. 873–90.

Laver, M. and Shepsle, K.A. (eds) (1994), *Cabinet Ministers and Parliamentary Government*, Cambridge University Press, New York.

Laver, M. and Shepsle, K.A. (1996), *Making and Breaking Governments: Cabinets and Legislatures in Parliamentary Democracies*, Cambridge University Press, New York.

Lax, D.A. and Sebenius, J.K. (1991), 'Thinking Coalitionally: Party Arithmetic, Process Opportunism and Strategic Sequencing', in Young, H.P. (ed) *Negotiation Analysis*, University of Michigan Press, Ann Arbor, pp. 153–93.

Leiserson, M. (1966), *Coalitions in Politics*, PhD Dissertation, Yale University.

Luebbert, G.M. (1983), 'Coalition Theory and Government Formation in Multiparty Democracies', *Comparative Politics*, pp. 235–49.

Luebbert, G.M. (1984), 'A Theory of Government Formation', *Comparative Political Studies*, vol. 17, pp. 229–64.

Luebbert, G. (1986), *Comparative Democracy. Policymaking and Governing Coalitions in Europe and Israel*, Columbia University Press, New York.

Luykx, Th. (1973), *Politieke Geschiedenis van België*, Elsevier, Brussel.

Luykx, Th. (1978), *Politieke Geschiedenis van België*, Elsevier, Brussel, second edition.

Luykx, Th. and Platel, M. (1985), *Politieke Geschiedenis van België*, Elsevier, Brussel.

Lijphart, A. (1968), *The Politics of Accommodation. Pluralism and Democracy in the Netherlands*, University of California Press, Berkely.

Lijphart, A. (1999), *Patterns of Democracy. Government Forms and Performance in Thirty-Six Countries*, Yale University Press, New Haven.

Maas, P.F. (1982), *Kabinetsformaties 1959–1973*, Sdu, 's-Gravenhage.

Nederlandse Staatscourant (1981–98), Dutch newspaper.

Müller, W.C. and Strøm, K. (eds) (2000), *Coalition Governments in Western Europe*, Oxford University Press, Oxford.

Neels, L. (1975), 'Regeringsverklaringen en Regeerakkoorden als Documenten van Toenemend Publiekrechtelijk Belang. Een Nieuwe Bron van het Publiek Recht?, *Rechtskundig Weekblad*, vol. 38, pp. 2369–410.

North, D.C. (1990), *Institutions, Institutional Change, and Economic Performance*, Cambridge University Press, New York.

Nousiainen, J. (1993), 'Decision-Making, Policy Content and Conflict Resolution in Western European Cabinets', in Blondel, J. and Müller-Rommel, F. (eds), *Governing Together. The Extent and Limits of Joint Decision-Making in Western European Cabinets*, Macmillan, London, pp. 259–82.

NRC Handelsblad, Dutch newspaper.

Peterson, R.L. and De Ridder, M.M. (1986), 'Government Formation As a Policy-Making Arena', *Legislative Studies Quarterly*, vol. 11, pp. 565–81.

Peterson, R.L., De Ridder, M.M., Hobbs, J.D. and McClellan, E.F. (1983), 'Government Formation and Policy Formulation. Patterns in Belgium and the Netherlands', *Res Publica*, 1983, pp. 49–82.

Platel, M. (1978), 'Van Stuyvenberg naar de Wetstraat 16. Een Derde Onderhandelingsronde over het Gemeenschapsakkoord', *Res Publica*, pp. 447–55.

Pridham, G. (ed) (1986), *Coalitional Behaviour in Theory and Practice. An Inductive Model for Western Europe*, Cambridge University Press, Cambridge.

Riker, W.H. (1962), *The Theory of Political Coalitions*, Yale University Press, New Haven.

Riker, W.A. (1986), *The Art of Political Manipulation*, Yale University Press, New Haven.

Rose, R. (1984), *Do Parties Make a Difference?*, Macmillan, London.

Sanders, D. and Herman, V. (1977), 'The Stability and Survival of Governments in Western Europe', *Acta Politica*, vol. 12, pp. 346–77.

Scharpf, F.W. (1997), *Games Real Actors Play. Actor-Centered Institutionalism in Policy Research*, Westview Press, Boulder.

Schofield, N. (1993), 'Political Competition and Multiparty Coalition Governments', *European Journal of Political Research*, vol. 23, pp. 1–33.

Strøm, K. (1984), 'Minority Governments in Parliamentary Democracies: The Rationality of Non-Winning Cabinet Solutions', *Comparative Political Studies*, vol. 17, pp. 199–227.

Strøm, K. (1990), *Minority Government and Majority Rule*, Cambridge University Press, Cambridge.

Strøm, K., Budge, I. and Laver, M.J. (1994), 'Constraints on Cabinet Formation in Parliamentary Democracies', *American Journal of Political Science*, vol. 38, pp. 303–35.

Strøm, K. and Müller, W.C. (2001) 'Coalition Agreements and Governance', paper presented at the American Political Science Association, San Fransisco, 29 August–2 September 2001.

Strøm, K., Müller, W.C. and Bergman, T. (eds) (forthcoming), *Coalition Governance in Parliamentary Democracies*, Oxford University Press, Oxford.

Timmermans, A. (1994), 'Cabinet Ministers and Policymaking in Belgium: The Impact of Coalition Constraints', in Laver, M. and Shepsle, K.A. (eds), *Cabinet Ministers and Parliamentary Government*, Cambridge University Press, New York, pp. 106–24.

Timmermans, A. (1998), 'Policy Conflicts, Agreements, and Coalition Governance', *Acta Politica*, vol. 33, pp. 409–32.

Timmermans, A. (1999), 'Regeerakkoorden, Conflicten en het Explosiegevaar in Coalities', *Beleid en Maatschappij*, vol. 26, pp. 78–88.

Timmermans, A. (2001), 'Arenas as Institutional Sites for Policymaking: Patterns and Effects in Comparative Perspective', *Journal of Comparative Policy Analysis*, vol. 3, pp. 311–37.

Timmermans, A. and Andeweg, R.B. (2000), 'The Netherlands: Still the Politics of Accommodation?', in Müller, W.C. and Strøm, K. (eds), *Coalition Governments in Western Europe*, Oxford University Press, Oxford, pp. 356–98.

Tops, P. and Dittrich, K. (1992), 'The Role of Policy in Dutch Coalition Building 1947–1981', in Laver, M.J. and Budge, I. (eds), *Party Policy and Government Coalitions*, St. Martin's Press, New York, pp. 277–311.

Trouw (1994–98), Dutch newspaper.

Tsebelis, G. (1995), 'Decisionmaking in Political Systems: Veto Players in Presidentialism, Parliamentarism, Multicameralism, and Multipartyism', *British Journal of Political Science*, vol. 25, pp. 289–325.

Van Tijn, J. and Van Weezel, M. (1986), *Inzake het Kabinet-Lubbers*, Sijthoff, Amsterdam.

Williamson, O.E. (1985), *The Economic Institutions of Capitalism*, Cambridge University Press, New York.

Warwick, P. (1979), 'The Durability of Coalition Governments in Parliamentary Democracies', *Comparative Political Studies*, vol. 11, pp. 465–98.

Warwick, P.V. (1994), *Government Survival in Parliamentary Democracies*, Cambridge University Press, New York.

Index